on track ...

YES

every album, every song

Stephen Lambe

T0308313

sonicbondpublishing.com

on track ...
YES

every album, every song

Stephen Lambe

sonicbondpublishing.com

Sonicbond Publishing Limited
www.sonicbondpublishing.co.uk
Email: info@sonicbondpublishing.co.uk

First Published in the United Kingdom 2023
First Published in the United States 2023

British Library Cataloguing in Publication Data:
A Catalogue record for this book is available from the British Library

Copyright Stephen Lambe 2023

ISBN 978-1-78952-282-2

The right of Stephen Lambe to be identified
as the author of this work has been asserted by him
in accordance with the Copyright, Designs and Patents Act 1988.
All rights reserved. No part of this publication may be reproduced, stored in a
retrieval system or transmitted in any form or by any means, electronic, mechanical,
photocopying, recording or otherwise, without prior permission in writing from
Sonicbond Publishing Limited

Typeset in ITC Garamond Std & ITC Avant Garde Gothic
Printed and bound in England

Graphic design and typesetting: Full Moon Media

Follow us on social media:
Twitter: https://twitter.com/SonicbondP
Instagram: www.instagram.com/sonicbondpublishing_/
Facebook: www.facebook.com/SonicbondPublishing/

Linktree QR code:

For Chris Squire, Alan White and Peter Banks

Acknowledgements

Special thanks also to Oliver Wakeman, Jon Anderson
and Bill Bruford for occasional moments of insight.

Thanks to Bruce Strickland for sharing his
ticket stubs and Yes programmes.

Thanks, as ever, to the Prog Widow – my gorgeous wife Gill.

Preface To The Revised Edition

Yes on track was first published towards the end of 2018, and has remained a best seller for Sonicbond Publishing ever since. However, it came out when we were still experimenting with the format of the series, and in the intervening years, the On Track have smartened up considerably, so it seemed like a good idea to revisit the book from scratch as it approaches its fifth anniversary.

I have revisited every sentence – though I've not necessarily changed words that (arguably) didn't need it. I've expanded the live albums section somewhat in the wake of other authors who have looked at this area with other artists rather more successfully than I did the first time around. I've also delved briefly into the 1975-76 solo albums period. On a few occasions, I've made substantive changes to some of the opinions I've previously expressed. Like all Yes fans, I've carried on listening over the last five years, and so I've amended some thoughts where my views have changed along the way.

In 2018, even the most optimistic of Yes fan had probably assumed that the band's recording years were over. Who would have predicted two brand-new albums, plus a mini album of material recorded around 2010? Both *The Quest* and *From A Page* appeared in recent reprints of the first edition of this book, but this edition also features 2023s *Mirror To The Sky* for the very first time.

Finally, the colour section has been revised from scratch to take into account Sonicbond's current house style.

When the book was first published, the band had just celebrated 50 years of existence. It seemed like a big deal at the time, but after five years, memories of that momentous event have faded slightly, so I have de-emphasised the anniversary in this edition. After all, 55 years on and counting, the band and various former members remain as active as ever. While it cannot go on forever, the band's 'indian summer' looks set to burn on for a while yet.

Stephen Lambe, July 2023

on track ...
YES

Contents

Introduction

Was there ever such a complex band as Yes?

By that, of course, I mean structurally complex. I can think of few groups that have had so many line-up changes, and yet so many members that have left the band and later rejoined; a band that have had so many different methodologies and motivations for creating music; a band that has been so divided by inter-band politics and squabbles over money. Yet Yes are a group of musicians that, at their best, have made some of the most spectacular and uplifting music ever created. It makes for a colourful story and one that has lasted for over 55 years in one form or another. Only for a couple of barren years in the early 1980s was there no band called Yes at all, and while other periods have seen the band dormant, someone – somewhere – was holding the torch. Musicians were planning or talking or writing. And fans were waiting.

One of the crucial factors that made Yes the band it was, happened before they formed in London in early 1968, from the ashes of a psychedelic band called Mabel Greer's Toyshop. Aside from drummer Bill 'Tubs' Bruford – who found his way into the band by the sheer weight of his talent as an eighteen-year-old – the band that formed was made up of relatively seasoned musicians. Tony Kaye was 22. Chris Squire and Peter Banks – who had already played together in the band The Syn – were both twenty but had played in professional groups since 1965. Jon Anderson had survived a lengthy stint in touring band The Warriors, but had also recorded a couple of singles under the name Hans Christian. He was a positively elderly 23. The band already had some chops, and while there was much still to learn, the individual musicians could play together safe in the knowledge of each other's competence.

Those levels of competence were soon to be tested, however. On the first two albums, the listener can almost feel Yes finding their feet and prodding at the limits of what was possible in popular music. Although only a limited success, the use of the orchestra on *Time And A Word* was at least ambitious, an attempt to try something new. It is no surprise that the impetus to do this came from Anderson, the visionary 'Napoleon' with the unusual voice and an even more unusual view of the world. In Squire and Bruford, the band already had a world-class rhythm section, and so much more than a standard bass and drums duo.

But what of the other two? Kaye was a talented and dextrous player but rather rooted – at this stage at least – to the jazz/blues organ stylings of the 1960s. In most bands, Peter Banks would have been the star, yet in Yes, he didn't quite cut the mustard, replaced in 1970 by another musician of astonishing ability in Steve Howe.

Kaye hung around for the ground-breaking *Yes Album*, the band's breakthrough record in the UK, a hybrid of the progressive rock the band were beginning to pioneer and other more derivative styles, but the arrival of Rick Wakeman for *Fragile* opened doors to much bolder styles of music, with instruments like the Moog and the Mellotron played not as novelty items but as key instruments in an ever-expanding palette of sounds. By *Close To The Edge* this transition was complete, with the band producing one of the defining albums of the early 1970s, taking the record-buying public on the same journey wherever the listeners were in the world.

Bruford departed for King Crimson – chasing the art rather than the money – and was replaced by the impressively hard-hitting and mobile Alan White (imagine Buddy Rich replaced by Animal from The Muppets). But lengthy tours and a ground-breaking triple live album and film in *Yessongs*, continued the momentum as Yes became one of the biggest bands in the world. It is likely that this momentum was slowed by the release of the bold but (arguably) inconsistent *Tales From Topographic Oceans*, leading to Wakeman's departure and the recruitment of the equally extravagant and talented Patrick Moraz. 1974's *Relayer* was even bolder, if anything – a real 'fuck you' to those that had criticised *Tales*, and with 1975 and 1976 taken up by touring, the money kept rolling in.

1976 saw the next line-up change, which was motivated as much by management needs and the rather less-than-savoury financial aspects of the band, as by musical considerations. Moraz was out – fired while rehearsing in his own country, no less – and Wakeman was back. His performance on *Going For The One* as a glorified session man was exemplary, and everyone else was also on fine form in this excellent album, largely made up of shorter pieces, but topped off by the astonishing, 15-minute 'Awaken'. Less so the patchy *Tormato,* which saw the band beginning to fragment again and then break apart completely in Paris at the end of 1979.

Howe, White and Squire continued with the fiery *Drama* bolstered by British pop duo (and self-confessed Yes fans) the Buggles – Trevor Horn and Geoff Downes – in a band now called by its detractors (not to mention a fair few fans), as The Yuggles. After a difficult tour with an inexperienced Horn struggling both vocally and with the 'sin' of not being Jon Anderson, the band called it a day. However, the Yes 'brand' was revived in 1983 when management once again saw pound signs by tagging on Jon Anderson onto an existing Squire/White project with South African guitarist Trevor Rabin and a returning Tony Kaye, called Cinema. Against the odds, *90125* was a huge success, bolstered by 'Owner Of A Lonely Heart', a number one single in the USA and a spectacular world tour. But they failed to capitalise, taking too long to produce a rather soulless and over-produced follow-up in *Big Generator*. Anderson jumped ship for the second time.

What came next may have felt unsavoury at the time. Anderson formed his own alternative 'Yes' using a band of cast-offs (if one were to put it unkindly) or the musicians that many felt should have been in Yes all along (to be more charitable). The resulting band was pretty decent, with Bill Bruford, in particular, invigorating and invigorated with his banks of electronic percussion, even if the sounds he created with it have dated somewhat. However, with Yes still technically existing on the west coast of America, a reckoning was sure to come, and come it did. The lawyers and managers got their heads together and created an eight-headed monster. If the album, *Union*, was a variable and often unsatisfactory beast, the tour itself was rather better, getting the best of its cast of thousands (well, eight).

What next?

Howe, Wakeman and Bruford were out again, and while the next album and tour saw a return to the *90125* line up – with an eye to the charts, one suspects – the spark failed to ignite a return to past glories. First, there was oblivion, then a glimmer of hope as the *Going For The One* line-up had another go, this time via an attempt to recapture the long-form glories of the early 1970s via *The Keys To Ascension* albums. However, by this time it was 1996 and the band were starting to chase shadows as one strange management decision followed another. If *Open Your Eyes*, with new young blood Billy Sherwood and Igor Khoroshev on board, was a bit of a bodge, they followed that with their last attempt to be 'new' and 'relevant' via the *The Ladder* album.

The shows supporting that patchy record was arguably their last attempt to 'tour' a brand new album, and the line-up changes continued into the 2000s. After the *Magnification* album – good but largely ignored – which took advantage of a lack of a keyboard player by replacing the role with an orchestra – and the subsequent Symphonic Tour, Wakeman returned in 2003. If the 1990s were about the attempt to recapture past glories, then the early 2000s were about the band becoming comfortable in its own skin, happy to recreate the past. The 2004 world tour, though, exhausted everyone, particularly Anderson. A 40th Anniversary Tour was planned in 2008, but with Anderson having suffered severe respiratory problems and Wakeman fearing what another long-term tour might do to his own health, first Oliver Wakeman (Rick's eldest son, with a playing style similar to his old man) and then French-Canadian singer Benoît David were recruited. Many fans cried foul. This was poor treatment of the man that represented the soul of the band, they said, with some justification.

Nonetheless, the band continued to tour led by Squire, Howe and White, even planning new material. The resulting album *Fly From Here,* which saw the younger Wakeman replaced by Geoff Downes, returning after 30 years, was co-ordinated by Trevor Horn, and saw Horn and Downes providing a lot of the songs, most of it written in the early 1980s. This was a smart move – a new Yes album with strong, older material. However, with David also out eventually – another victim of a band unwilling to lose momentum while a band member suffered health issues – and excellent new singer Jon Davison recruited, the band continued to tour and had one more album in it, the tired and poorly received *Heaven and Earth*.

There were several more stings in the tail, however. The health of neither Squire nor White held up. Chris Squire suffered from a rare form of

Leukaemia and, in 2015, became the second member of the Yes family to pass away, following Peter Banks in 2013. White's health problems were kept very private, and while he remained a talismanic figure, he clearly could not play as he used to, and sadly he, too, passed away in 2022. Billy Sherwood had been personally recruited by Squire, while White's replacement was a no-brainer, as Jay Schellen had been filling in with the band for some years anyway. Of the Yes that keeps things going, only a sprightly Howe remaines, and once again, Anderson – a rejuvenated figure into his late 70s – looks happy to be playing Yes music. He did this first in a short-lived Brian Lane-managed project called Anderson, Rabin, Wakeman – featuring Trevor and Rick. This project was later cheekily called Yes, before folding in 2018, having failed to release a promised new album. Later, Anderson toured both with The Paul Green School of Rock (a group of music students) and The Band Geeks (a band of Yes-literate US-based musicians).

But this is the story of how each album was created and how the fundamental battle between musical innovation and commerciality was won – or lost – in each case. Yes are my favourite band, and I am naturally well-disposed towards anything they do. Yet I have tried to stay as objective as possible when assessing the music. All creators of art have peaks and troughs, and Yes' graph would put the Himalayas to shame. Let's ascend and descend together.

Notes

Somebody somewhere will write a book about every live version and every other variation of every Yes track. This is not that book, and I have only referred to versions when I believe they add something to our understanding of the album in question. Many of the Rhino remasters have 'studio run-throughs' of some pieces, particularly the epics. I have not mentioned them here. In addition, you will find that this book is a bootleg-free zone. Dozens of bootlegs of the band – good and bad – have been released over the years, and, aside from the moral considerations, there is simply too much material to examine. The only exception to this is the BBC Recording of the Wembley Arena concerts in 1978. This has been mined for a few 'official' live tracks over the years, and I hope that we will see an 'official' release of the full set sometime in the future.

Nobody's perfect, least of all me, and If I have missed anything out that I really shouldn't have, then do contact me via the publishers so I can correct it for future editions. An email address can be found at the end of this book.

Cast of Characters

I cannot think of another major rock band that has had so many line up changes. Even though King Crimson have reinvented themselves many times over the years, their line ups always revolve around one man, Robert Fripp. In the case of Yes, these changes have generally been more gradual, built around a group of musicians rather than just one. Until his death in June 2015, only Chris Squire had been in every incarnation of the 'official' band. Overall, eighteen musicians have been 'official' members of Yes, so what follows are brief thumbnail sketches of them all.

Only 'full' members of the band have been included. Even this is moot, since some members were probably on contracts rather than considered 'permanent'. My definition, therefore, is any musician that played live and was also involved in creating new music in the studio. Guests, stand-by and touring musicians – for instance, Tom Brislin, Lou Molinaro III, Adam Wakeman and Lee Pomeroy – have been omitted. Tony Levin has a better claim for full membership due to his participation in *Union* but has not been included, and I have also left out Eddie Jobson, who joined briefly in 1983 when Kaye left but decided not to stay. I have considered the band dissolved between 1980 and 1983, and despite my inclusion of the album in this book, participation in ABWH is not considered to be membership of Yes.

Jon Anderson (born 1944)

Vocals, harp, guitar, percussion.
1968-1980, 1983-1988, 1991- 2008, 2017-2018 (ARW)
Born in Accrington, Lancashire, Anderson is felt by many fans to be the 'soul' of Yes, not only for his lyrics but also for his overall orchestration of the fortunes and music of the band, particularly in the early days. His relatively meagre skills as a musician set him apart from the virtuosity of the rest of the group, but his musical vision – as well as his unusual worldview – makes him one of the most singular musicians of his generation. And then, of course, there is 'that' voice – his unique alto. He has rarely had problems with his voice and pitching (ie. singing the right note) has not been an issue since decent onstage monitoring became a 'thing' in the early 1970s. If you consider all those live recordings, he doesn't always sound like his voice is in great shape – perhaps too many dates into a long tour – but does he sing the wrong note? Never.

Outside Yes, Anderson has had a varied solo career, and not always a successful one. He supposedly has as many projects unfinished as he has finished. He enjoyed a short but interesting career as a vocalist for hire in the 1980s, and his most prolific time as a solo artist was the early to mid-1990s. However, it was his career with Greek keyboard player Vangelis – himself one of the great sonic stylists of the 1970s and 1980s – that gave him the greatest success outside Yes. The duo released four studio albums and had two massive hit singles in the UK with 'I Hear You Now' and 'I'll Find My Way Home'.

As for Yes, Anderson is a quirky character and supposedly not always easy to work with, and his relationships with Squire and Howe, in particular, were caught up, not just (allegedly) in financial squabbles but also in personality issues that blighted the band from the late 1970s onwards. Yet Anderson remains the most beloved of the Yes family, and it's not hard to understand why.

Chris Squire (born 1948, died 2015)
Bass, vocals, piano
1968 -1980, 1983-2015

Apart from Anderson, Squire is always considered the keeper of the Yes flame, and his death in June 2015 was met with understandable grief by many thousands worldwide. His nickname 'Fish' (not to be confused with the erstwhile Marillion vocalist) came (amongst other things) from his habit of taking enormously long baths. He was also constantly, and famously, late for everything. A chorister in his youth in London, Squire was tall, elegant and good-looking, with big hands that earmarked him for life as a bassist. However, he came at his chosen instrument from a supremely melodic angle, almost (but not quite) as a lead instrument. For me, his playing is a hybrid of the traditional bassist role – providing the 'bottom' – and a lead instrumentalist – giving the band unusual options when looking for that extra texture in an arrangement.

He usually played with a pick and his main instrument – the Rickenbacker bass with it famously accentuated 'high end' – meant that he cut through the mix better than most bassists. In a nutshell, he is one of the most 'heard' bassists in history, with a technique completely different to the jazz-orientated players so popular in the 1970s. His strong backing vocals, which complimented Anderson's so well, were also a crucial part of the band's character, particularly in a live setting.

Unlike Anderson, most of Squire's work was within Yes. He released a superb solo album, *Fish Out Of Water* in 1975, and his collaboration with Billy Sherwood produced a couple of decent rock albums, too. But Squire will always be associated with Yes above anything – and almost anybody – else.

Peter Banks (born 1947, died 2013)
Guitar, vocals
1968-1970

Banks was the first musician to leave Yes – ousted by Anderson and Squire – and it is clear that the anger and disappointment this produced never left him throughout what was a stop-start musical career. A talented and versatile player in his own right, he went on to form the groups Flash and Empire. Both bands showed promise but never fulfilled their potential, and his solo album *Two Sides Of Peter Banks* – which included a guest appearance by Jan Akkerman of Focus – also failed to live up to expectations. The debut album by Flash – released in 1972 – is a rather spooky 'alternative Yes'. It features a more primitive progressive rock, looser and a little bluesier, considering that by that time, Yes, were recording the groundbreaking *Close To The Edge*.

Banks had a career revival in the 1990s and 2000s as a solo artist and also in the improvisatory trio Harmony In Diversity, but these projects never rose above cult status. He was involved in early discussions to take part in revivals of both The Syn (with whom he had played with Squire prior to Yes) and also Flash but was ultimately excluded from both projects. His 2001 memoir *Beyond And Before* is an excellent read. Many of his recordings have been reassessed in recent years, and several have reappeared via the excellent Esoteric label. They are worth checking out.

Bill Bruford (born 1949)
Drums, Percussion.
1968-1972, 1991-1992

It's hard not to admire this most enigmatic of percussionists. Born in Surrey to a relatively well-off, middle-class family, Bruford has had a hugely varied and creative career, contrasting extreme pragmatism in terms of his financial and organisational affairs, with a desire to chase the art rather than untold riches. He developed his studied and very musical style of drumming while in Yes, then mystified the band by leaving just as the group were about to 'make it big' to join King Crimson. He also pioneered the use of electronic drums in the 1980s via a long-standing relationship with manufacturer Simmons, a texture he brought to Anderson, Bruford, Wakeman, Howe and his brief tenure back in Yes thereafter. However, for me, it is his solo band – Bruford – that was his most successful, musically, mixing jazz with rock in a very British-sounding fusion.

Later years were spent teaching and mainly playing the music that is his first love – jazz – via his band Earthworks, but there were many other, relatively low-key projects until his retirement in 2009. He has since refused to return to exhibit his own perceived decline in musical powers in front of thousands of people per night for large amounts of money. Unlike other members of Yes, Bruford has always had an unusually balanced view of his life and a return to playing seems very unlikely. I admire him for that.

Tony Kaye (born 1946)
Keyboards.
1968-1970, 1983-1995

Handsome, enigmatic and private, Tony Kaye is probably the most underrated musician in the Yes family. The first two Yes albums show him to be a dexterous and inventive player, particularly on his favoured instrument, the organ.

However, he seemed intimidated by the arrival of Steve Howe in 1970 and lost his place, as much for his unwillingness to embrace the new orchestral direction of that band, as for any perceived lack of technique. Yet he has spent more time in Yes than Rick Wakeman, even if – during the *90125 / Big Generator* era – he was little more than a live keyboardist, with Trevor Rabin playing many of the keyboards on those albums.

When outside Yes, he formed the band Badger, played live with David Bowie and performed a lot of sessions, going 'off radar' for years at a time. He also formed a strong friendship with Billy Sherwood, playing with him in the band Circa and also touring with him as a duo. When the band received their Rock and Roll Hall Of Fame award in 2017, he was the only living member of the band not to attend. He was involved in the 50th-anniversary celebrations and released his first solo album, *The End of Innocence*, in 2021.

Steve Howe (born 1947)
Guitars, vocals.
1970-1980, 1991-1992, 1996-

There is little doubt that Howe is one of the most inventive and distinctive guitarists of his generation, with a style almost perfect for Yes. With his trademark hollow-body Gibson and his myriad of influences – including Wes Montgomery and Les Paul – no guitarist sounds like Howe. He has kept himself fit over the years, too, and seems to be playing as well as ever, technically, but without the fire of the early 70s. Howe's solo career has been interesting and pretty high on quality, whether playing full-on rock, or acoustic pieces, and he
has not been afraid to tour small venues on his own. He is an intense character who protects his hands and as a result can come off as reserved, he also retains his almost child-like love of music, as his large guitar collection demonstrates. His autobiography All My Yesterdays was published in 2021 and demonstrated his precision and love of the guitar far more than his desire to dish the dirt on his bandmates.

Beyond Yes, he was a founder member of two bands that attempted a more commercial style of rock. Firstly Asia – the hugely-successful supergroup with John Wetton, Carl Palmer and Geoff Downes – and then GTR. This latter project was an attempt to link two guitar-playing Steves – Howe and Hackett – into a viable group, but with less success than Asia. Anderson, Bruford, Wakeman, Howe probably came at the right time for him, as did the invitation to rejoin Yes in 1996. Unusually, he has also embraced the 'tribute band' culture, playing live with the UK-based Yes tribute Fragile with some success in the mid-2000s.

Rick Wakeman (born 1949)
Keyboards
1971-1974, 1976-1980, 1991-1992, 1996-1997, 2003-2004, 2017-2018 (ARW)
Wakeman's career is impossible to summarise in a single paragraph. By the time he joined Yes in 1971 he had already been a member of the Strawbs, played on countless recording sessions, including 'Space Oddity' and much of

Hunky Dory by David Bowie. Between periods in Yes, he became a huge solo star via a string of albums on the A&M label, such as *The Six Wives Of Henry Eighth* and *Journey To The Centre Of The Earth*, a number one hit album in the UK. Life wasn't always so kind. He struggled with alcoholism and has married four times. He had his first heart attack in 1974. He has had various businesses over the years, and put financial backing into the short-lived Mellotron update, the Birotron, but otherwise has had a close association with the Moog organisation and Japanese company Korg.

In recent years, he has had a parallel career as a comedian and raconteur. He has combined occasional full-band events with the English Rock Ensemble with piano-and-story theatre tours, telling colourful tales from his long life on the road. His performance of 'Life On Mars' following the death of David Bowie touched millions in the UK, and led to an unintended upswing in his fortunes as a popular pianist. In his 70s, his prodigious technique has never escaped him, and he remains as consistent and flamboyant a performer as ever.

Alan White (1949-2022)
Drums, percussion, piano, vocals
1972-1980, 1983-2022

Although only 23 when he joined Yes, White – originally from the North East of England – had already played with John Lennon's Plastic Ono Band, Alan Price and Balls with Denny Laine. Like Squire, most of his energies since have been devoted to Yes, although he released two solo albums, one of which turned into a short-lived band, White. He also played with various bands in the Seattle area – where he lived until his death – and was also in Circa with Billy Sherwood. Around 1981, White joined Squire in the short-lived XYZ with Jimmy Page of Led Zeppelin, before forming Cinema with Trevor Rabin, later to become – once again – Yes. His power and energy in the 1970s was astonishing, as live recordings and videos demonstrate. Problems with his health in recent years diminished his powers as a drummer, although he did play on *The Quest* and he passed away in 2022.

Patrick Moraz (born 1948)
Keyboards
1974-1976

Swiss keyboard wizard Moraz was the perfect choice to replace Rick Wakeman. He had previously played in the Swiss-based band Mainhorse and then Refugee, effectively the Nice but with Moraz replacing Keith Emerson. He fitted the bill with Yes perfectly as his interest in jazz suited the direction of the band as they composed material for *Relayer*. After Yes, he had a prodigious solo career, mixing musical styles including rock, jazz, electronica and South American music. He also had a piano and drum duo with Bill Bruford in the 1980s. Although he left Yes under strange circumstances, he continues a broad association with the band, appearing onstage during the 2018 50th anniversary celebrations and also appearing at *Cruise To The Edge*, the yearly Yes-organised pleasure cruise.

Trevor Horn (born 1949)
Vocals, bass
1980-1981
Trevor's time as a member of Yes was only part of an association that led to him producing the *90125* album, and working on the initial sessions for *Big Generator*. Originally the bassist and vocalist of The Buggles with Geoff Downes, Horn went on to produce countless top pop acts, including ABC, Frankie Goes To Hollywood, Art Of Noise and Dollar, and formed label ZTT with journalist Paul Morley. He is one of two members of the Yes family to have been honoured by the British establishment (the other being Rick Wakeman), having been given a CBE for services to the music industry.

Geoff Downes (born 1952)
Keyboards, vocals
1980-1981, 2011-
Initially associated with Horn in The Buggles, the two went their separate ways after the *Drama* Tour. Downes formed Asia with Steve Howe, John Wetton and Carl Palmer, catapulting them all to further success in the 1980s. Downes was the one constant member of Asia throughout the 1980s and 1990s, but he also worked as a producer for The Thompson Twins and GTR. He has also produced the occasional low-key solo album and also formed an Asia side-project called Icon with his long-term writing partner John Wetton in the 2000s. More recently, he formed a project with singer Chris Braide called the Downes Braide Association.

The original line up of Asia re-united in 2006, and Downes also re-joined Yes in 2011. Remaining keyboard player in Yes is not an easy task, and Downes had proved surprisingly adept at playing in the styles of his predecessors, for which he should receive great credit.

Trevor Rabin (born 1954)
Guitar, keyboards, vocals
1983-1995, 2017-2018 (ARW)
Rabin was a teen idol – and guitar prodigy – in his native South Africa via his band Rabbitt. Moving to London at the end of the 1970s, Rabin released three solo albums in the heavy rock / AOR vein, tapping into the spirit of the New Wave Of British Heavy Metal, also producing albums by Wild Horses and Manfred Mann's Earth Band during this time. A move to Los Angeles saw various opportunities come and go (including the chance to be in Asia) – but he eventually found a path to Squire and White, and the rest (as they say) is history.

After an excellent solo album in 1988 called *Can't Look Away*, Rabin found himself involved in film scores and recording, something which has taken up most of his professional life. In 2013 he released a very varied album of instrumentals *Jacaranda*, and of course, returned to Yes music via the Anderson, Rabin, Wakeman version in 2016. Another solo album was expected in 2023.

Billy Sherwood (born 1965)

Guitar, Bass, Keyboards, Vocals
1998-2000, 2015-

California-based multi-instrumentalist Sherwood has been part of the Yes family since working on 'The More We Live, Let Go' with Squire for the Union album, although his band World Trade had some minor success around the same time. He played back up guitar and sang on the *Talk* tour, and was part of the production team for *The Keys To Ascension 2*, before becoming a full-time member in 1997 when further tracks he was working on with Squire became the basis for *Open Your Eyes*. He stayed in the band for *The Ladder* and both tours in support of those albums. He departed in 2000, returning first to record the backing vocals on the Heaven and Earth album, then on bass in 2015 following Squire's death, a move universally praised by those fans who wanted the band to continue.

Aside from his prolific solo output, Sherwood has formed a few bands based around the Yes family, including Circa with Kaye and initially White, not to mention Conspiracy with Squire plus Yoso with former Toto vocalist Bobby Kimball. He is also the main instigator behind Arc of Life with Jon Davison. He performed with Asia after the death of John Wetton and he has even recorded with Star Trek legend William Shatner.

Igor Khoroshev (born 1965)

Keyboards, vocals
1998-2000

A flamboyant character and performer, Russian Khoroshev moved to the USA in the 1990s, where he met Anderson while working for a software company. Since leaving Yes after the Masterworks Tour in 2000, after an incident concerning a female security guard, he has continued to work in soundtracks. Clearly very talented, he might be considered a sad loss to the progressive rock world, and one wonders what he might have achieved had he stayed in the band.

Oliver Wakeman (born 1972)

Keyboards
2008-2011

The eldest son of Rick Wakeman, Oliver joined Yes on his father's suggestion in 2008, after a career as a keyboard player recording albums with Steve Howe,

Clive Nolan of Arena and Pendragon, and with his own band. Ousted during the initial sessions for *Fly From Here*, some of the songs he was working on for Yes wound up on the excellent *Ravens And Lullabies*, an album recorded with legendary guitarist Gordon Giltrap in 2013. The author had the pleasure of assisting Oliver and Gordon with the promotional live tour for that album in 2014. Oliver makes a couple of small contributions to *Fly From Here,* but otherwise, the only record of his time in Yes for a while was the *In the Present – Live From Lyon* double live album. However, Oliver shocked Yes fans worldwide in 2020 with the release of From A Page, a short album of Yes tracks resurrected from the initial *Fly From Here* sessions.

Benoît David (born 1966)
Vocals
2008-2012
French Canadian singer Benoît David was recruited from the Yes tribute band Close To The Edge in 2008. At the same time, he was the vocalist with Quebec-based band Mystery, singing on three albums. His voice was in a similar register to Anderson but quite distinctive, and later tours saw him developing further as a vocalist, as is shown on *Fly From Here*. Following his experience with Yes, he retired from singing and has yet to re-emerge.

Jon Davison (born 1971)
Vocals, guitar
2012 onwards
Davison also played in a Yes tribute (called Roundabout) but became a member of Yes via a more circuitous route. He was spotted by US band Glass Hammer, and sang for them on several albums, only leaving in 2014 when his Yes commitments became too arduous. When David was ousted after a period of poor health which affected his singing, there was a mad rush to find Davison to fulfil Yes tour commitments, having been suggested via Taylor Hawkins of the Foo Fighters, a mutual friend of both Davison and Squire. He is an excellent fit for Yes – an able and confident live singer with a voice close to Anderson's, yet not so close as to be unable to perform Horn material.

Jay Schellen (born 1960)
Drums, percussion
2023 – (officially)
Jay played drums with Yes when Alan White's health issues made it impossible for him to play entire shows from 2016. It wasn't until early 2023 that he was confirmed as the band's official drummer. He had long been associated with Yes, having played with Billy Sherwood actross various projects since the late 1980s.

Yes Cover Art

Roger Dean

The name Roger Dean is synonymous with Yes, and in the same way that the band's music has been much imitated, so has Dean's unique cover art and typography. With his remarkable curved Yes logo, with the 'tail' of the Y winding like a snake though the E and becoming the S from the bottom, he created one of the most iconic pieces of graphic art in rock music history.

Most bands change their typography over time, as indeed Yes did, but nobody returned to one design, indeed one artist, as much as Yes have done over the 50 years plus since *Close to the Edge* was released. A myriad of other bands have used his art as a template for their own work. His designs have inspired books and movies, too, as those that have seen the huge Hollywood hit *Avatar* will testify.

The amiable and gentlemanly Dean designed the covers for an astonishing number of Yes albums, although not all of these albums are the best Yes recordings and not all of these covers are his best work. Overall, his style can be considered 'fantasy art', but with many variations. Most recently, his work has moved towards fantastical landscapes with a greater realist edge. His paintings often play with perspective, so as the viewer looks closely at his pictures, we realise that what he is depicting isn't physically possible, or at least topographically unlikely. While Yes have never been a 'cool' band, Dean's imagery has flirted with fashion from time to time. Sarah Jessica Parker even wore a *Tales From Topographic Oceans* t-shirt on an episode of *Sex In the City* in the early 2000s, while Lady Gaga can be seen wearing a Yes t-shirt in the 2018 version of *A Star is Born*. As well as the iconic Yes logo, Dean's personal hallmark is the space craft depicted for *Fragile* – it appears whenever his name does on everything he designs.

It is four studio – and one live – albums for which Dean is most celebrated. Dean first worked with Yes after he sent a portfolio to Phil Carson at Atlantic records, who employed him to design the cover of *Fragile*. Taking the album title as his inspiration, Dean envisaged a tiny blue-green world in a dark blue void, with a strange spaceship flying away from it. On the cover, the world is intact; on the back, the world is beginning to break up. The vinyl version also includes a booklet with Dean's paintings on its cover. Many of Dean's favourite features are apparent immediately – his love of exotic trees in unusual situations and paths that curve in and out of the picture are a particular feature.

Close to the Edge was even bolder, if deceptively simple. The first Yes album to include the famous logo, the cover is a single burst of green, shifting from dark to light from top to bottom. The gatefold, however, features an astonishing landscape – waterfalls cascading from a lake on all sides of a mountain top. Where is the water coming from? A path snakes onto the lake from other mountain tops. Wherever you go in this world, you are ... Close To The Edge ...

Yessongs showed the eventual path of the fragments of the planet introduced in Fragile. For me, the brown front cover with its green tendrils of vegetation is his least successful. It is rather an odd mess, but the internal paintings are stunning, showing the segments travelling through space, landing in an alien sea and then in place in a misty landscape. Finally, we see the return of the spacecraft from the cover of *Fragile*.

If ever there was an album whose cover summed up and complimented its tone, it has to be the sumptuous gatefold painting that sits across the front and back of *Tales From Topographic Oceans*. The moon rises over an ancient pyramid. In the foreground, we see ancient stone piles, and yes, those are fish swimming through the atmosphere on the back cover. Deceptively simple yet awash with hints at mythology and evolution, it's a stunning piece of work. As is *Relayer*, a huge contrast, reflecting the war-like nature of the music. Two figures on horses ride into a huge cavern, while on the back, a snake curls menacingly. Does the snake represent evil? Aside from this detail, this is a Tolkien-esque image, yet its monochrome tones with just hints of colour in the snake are remarkable. This sort of cover is what vinyl was for. The listener has the music, they have the pictures and they have their imagination.

The late 70s Yes albums had covers controversially designed by Hipgnosis, the agency that had made iconic album covers for Pink Floyd, but Dean made a brief comeback with a superb cover for the second live album *Yesshows* in 1979 and a painting for the 1981 compilation *Classic Yes* – an odd cover, this one, with an almost photo-negative feel – returning properly to Yes studio albums for the *Drama* album in 1980. This painting is not my favourite, but it does have a sort of appropriate, almost abstract charm. His remarkable painting for *Anderson, Bruford, Wakeman, Howe* (1989) mixes the ancient with sci-fi using an almost photo-realist quality. This marks a period when Dean's paintings become decoration rather than an integral part of the album experience, with his name attached to a Yes-related project seemingly more important than the actual painting. That said, his two paintings for *Union* are very impressive in his fantastical landscape style. He repeated this approach equally impressively with his paintings for the two *Keys To Ascension* albums and by this time, Dean had become the reliable backstop for Yes. The band tried new cover art and artists on a regular basis, but when they needed a safety net and a reminder of past glories, Dean was there with another fine painting, and the fans were happy.

When the band started recording regular live albums in the new millennium, and released several official compilations, these always had a cover by Dean, and all the studio albums in the 2010 and 2020s, have fine Dean covers. *Heaven and Earth* has a very striking painting, a long way from his early work, yet with hints – in the shape of the mushroom cloud – of the planet fragments from *Yessongs*, while the splash of colour in the foreground is striking, almost jarring, as is the strange black and white colouring on the classic logo. Both *Fly From Here* and *Fly From Here – The Return Trip* have beautiful, green-based paintings suggesting the jungle, although they are very different illustrations, they have similar compositional styles – and different animals in the foreground.

Roger Dean did design another logo, a more angular design for the *Yesyears* compilation in 1991, and this hung around for a while, appearing on the *Keys to Ascension* albums (in parallel with the old logo) and *The Ladder* with the old logo totally absent, but again – it never quite captured the imagination, and by the time *Fly From Here* was released, the old logo was back on its own, remaining for *The Quest* and *Mirror To The Sky*.

Other cover art.

There was, of course, life before and between Roger Dean covers, and whenever the band felt the need to 're-invent' itself, Dean was ditched in favour of a new broom. *Yes* and *Time and a Word* were both given different covers for their UK and US releases. The first album has a simple 'speech bubble' design for the UK release, and a band picture for the USA, while the same pattern was repeated with *Time And A Word* – an odd and rather unsatisfyingly abstract design in the UK and a simple band picture (featuring Steve Howe, who is not on the album) in the USA. *The Yes Album* is distinctive, with its rather clichéd film-strip design and a low-light picture of the band and that disembodied mannequin head, which hung around as a band symbol for some time, even appearing on the *90125 Live* video. You also get Tony Kaye's ankle in a plaster cast. Roger Dean, however, arrived at the right time, just as the band were starting to make commercial headway.

The changes were well and truly rung in 1977 when, after almost three years without a new Yes album, the decision was made to use the Hipgnosis agency for *Going For The One*. This is a striking cover – almost as iconic as the Dean paintings – but it has dated rather badly. A naked man stares up at what appear to be skyscrapers against a blue sky, but we can see that these are actually just shapes masquerading as buildings, while various lines criss-cross the picture. As an image, it 'parallels' the aspirational nature of the title track while also suggesting the track which closes side one. It is daring and distinctive, and the same can also be said of the follow up cover for *Tormato*, although in a less impressive way. The title is a terrible pun, a play on Howe's chosen title YesTor (after the hill on Dartmoor, in Devon), and the tomato that was thrown at the intended album photograph out of desperation, after it was rejected by almost everyone. Incidentally, the tomato was almost certainly thrown by a Hipgnosis employee, rather than by Rick Wakeman, as is sometimes suggested. Dean was back for *Drama,* at a time when the band were searching for the familiar.

The sudden re-emergence of Yes in 1983 understandably brought about a complete re-invention of how the band was to be sold to the world, and the cover of *90125* is steeped in the quasi-modernist minimalism rife in 1980s design, with the cover shapes generated by computer. Unlike the music, thankfully. It's grey with some geometric colour patterns in the middle – and no Dean logo. The same approach was used for *Big Generator* – with its oblique reference to the *90125* cover, clearly intended as a new Yes logo of sorts. It didn't take, and Dean was back for *Union*.

Talk in 1994 saw the next attempt to bring the band up to date, this time with another minimalist cover, and a colourful, child-like logo from artist Peter Max (signed, no less). It's an attractive cover (albeit much disliked by some Yes fans) with great use of colour on the logo, but once again, with the relationship with Eagle Records abandoned and the line up dissolved after the *Talk* tour, Dean was back, and so was his logo. *Open Your Eyes* actually uses Dean's logo as the entire cover in a deeply unimaginative way. Presumably, the budget didn't stretch to a painting, while again, the cover of *Magnification* mixed the high-profile Dean logo with a rather dull, starry cover but some rather more interesting computer-generated designs within the CD booklet. And that was pretty much it – since the Symphonic DVD cover, nostalgia has been the name of the day, and it's been all Dean. At least, it was until, of course, Yes, featuring Anderson, Rabin and Wakeman appeared, without the rights to use the Dean logo.

Will it ever end?

Yes (1969)

Personnel:
Jon Anderson: vocals and incidental percussion
Chris Squire: bass, vocals
Peter Banks: guitar, vocals
Bill Bruford: drums, vibes
Tony Kaye: organ, piano
Produced at Advision and Trident studios London, March-April 1969 by Paul Clay and Yes
Release date: July 1969.
Highest Chart Places: None
Running time: 41:30

Yes was recorded just four months after a pivotal gig at the Royal Albert Hall supporting Cream in their farewell concert. The band were still in the process of developing as a live act, although intensive rehearsals had gone a long way towards honing their skills and they were developing a justified reputation as an exciting concert band, mixing re-invented, expanded cover versions with their own material. As a result, this first effort largely recreates the arrangements of many of the songs from that live set. Allocated Atlantic house producer Paul Clay – Jon Anderson had wanted Paul McCartney – the final album is not at all bad. Six – somewhat variable – original tracks combine with two cover versions to produce the final album, although several other songs were also recorded and appear on the 2003 Rhino re-master.

Musically, the record is an interesting mixture of styles – from the unashamedly psychedelic calling cards of the two opening tracks and the Beatles cover (on side two) to the somewhat cloying 'Yesterday and Today' and 'Sweetness'. 'Looking Around' was clearly intended as the 'big pop single', while the two most interesting tracks are the proto-Progressive Rock pieces 'Harold Land' and 'Survival'. It is not hard to work out why the band were so well thought of as a live act. Jon Anderson's voice was unique even then, and Chris Squire was already showing that swashbuckling bass style for which he became so famous. Bill Bruford comes across very much as the aspiring jazz man – very skilled yet not quite in possession of the precise style that was to make him so famous in the 1970s. As for the other musicians, Tony Kaye remains, for me, the unsung hero of both this and its follow-up *Time and a Word*. His organ playing is powerful, melodic and dextrous, and his reputation as a 'journeyman' rests largely on his relatively safe performance on *The Yes Album*, when stylistic changes within the band left him out on a limb. For me, the only weak link – and this is no more than a minor issue – is Peter Banks. His gimmicky guitar playing is jazzy and loose, a mixture of Pete Townsend and Wes Montgomery. It is perfectly fine for the material, but it is clear even at this stage that he was not really up to the ambitions of Anderson and Squire.

Despite some ambitious arrangements and some decent original material – particularly 'Survival', the one true classic here – it is not hard to see why the album failed to make the impression so many had hoped for it. There were a myriad of other bands doing things like this in 1969. But the promise of better to come was there.

'Beyond and Before' (Squire, Clive Bayley)

A single note guitar riff and a swirl of harmony vocals announce the band's first recorded song, written by Squire and Clive Bayley, a musician who had played in Squire's short-lived band Mabel Greer's Toyshop and who might have ended up in Yes. It's a psychedelic piece, with plenty of Beatles influences. There are no lead vocals – the three vocalists sing the whole piece in harmony. Also of note is Bruford's drumming – his snare work is much more complex than the norm for such a song. Peter Banks' guitar fills are fine, but no more than that. Nonetheless, it is an impressive start, and the quieter section towards the end shows how polished the band already were at controlling tempo and dynamics.

'I see you' (Jim McGuinn, David Crosby)

Banks is far more impressive in his clean jazz style at the start of this fine reworking of such a well-known Byrds song. Anderson gets his first lead vocal proper, although the harmonies are still prominent, as is Bruford's excellent cymbal work. It's a fast-paced piece, showing that the band could really rock out when needed. The guitar/drums duet mid-song – with Banks showing off his ability with the volume knob on his Rickenbacker – could apparently go on for ten minutes in a live setting. Thankfully, we get only a couple of minutes of it here, though once again, Bruford's jazz drumming is spectacular. It's another very solid track with a fine arrangement.

'Yesterday and Today' (Anderson)

Track three is far quieter, and Anderson gets to show us how good he is with a melody. He also double – or possibly triple – tracked his lead vocals, a technique for which he was to develop some ability. The arrangement is delicate, although not particularly well recorded or mixed, with some nice acoustic guitar work from Banks and some rare but welcome piano from Kaye.

'Looking Around' (Anderson, Squire)

Clearly slated to be a single, 'Looking Around' is the first attempt at 'the hit', and very fine it is, too. Kaye – so far buried in the mix somewhat on the album – is upfront with a splendidly bluesy organ riff and some nicely dexterous flourishes, not unlike Keith Emerson. The song itself is also good, mixing lead and harmony vocals beautifully, and the vocal melody is very reminiscent of Paul McCartney. The reverb on the vocals towards the end of the song is also a nice touch. The song really should have been a hit.

'Harold Land' (Anderson, Squire, Bruford)
Then, all of a sudden, we have progressive rock. The galloping intro to
the first track on side two – with Kaye dominant on both organ and piano
– sounds rather like *Nursery Cryme*-era Genesis, before straightening out
into a more conventional riff-heavy intro. Only the song itself disappoints
a rather overwrought sixties-style anti-war piece, where, for once, the
harmony vocals clutter the arrangement slightly. It's a bold track, and if, in
the end, the execution doesn't quite match the ambition, it's an interesting
sign of things to come. Bruford's writing credit is probably due to the fact
that he came up with the name of the protagonist. 'Harold Land' was the
name of a favourite jazzman. The – brief – fashion of naming songs after
fictitious people during the psychedelic era, typified by 'Eleanor Rigby', and
more importantly (one suspects) 'Arnold Layne' by Pink Floyd, released in
1967. Harold is a more sympathetic character than Arnold and his 'strange
hobby' (look it up).

'Every Little Thing' (John Lennon, Paul McCartney)
The explosive intro to this Beatles cover epitomises the power of the band,
with Banks 'wigging out' somewhat and Bruford bashing the living daylights
out of his kit. The main melody is introduced before the first vocal and
Banks also slips in a bit of the Beatles mega-hit 'Day Tripper', a playful
touch he rather liked. The harmony vocals on the chorus are spectacular,
and overall this is a worthy cover, possibly better than the original. The
band liked their arrangement enough to recreate it as an encore on the
2004 World Tour, although with only Anderson and Squire present from the
original recording.

'Sweetness' (Anderson, Squire, Clive Bailey)
The full band demonstrates that they can do 'delicate' as well as 'powerful' on
this rather sappy ballad, although the arrangement is lovely and the vocals
work well as you'd expect, with a nice 'build' towards the chorus. Choosing
this over 'Looking Around' as the first single was probably a mistake, as it
sank without trace.

'Survival' (Anderson)
Survival is much loved amongst Yes fans, and if the debut album has a
'classic' on it, this is it. The intro gives Squire his most obvious bass 'moment'
on the album before Kaye's terrific, slightly Eastern-sounding riff takes over as
the bass settles into a thunderous groove, punctuated with a lighter rendering
of the riff. This is a sensational opening, which then gives way to Anderson's
delicate verse. The build towards the chorus is beautifully handled and the
simple chorus itself is magical. The final few seconds of the song reprise the
intro playfully. A live video version of this song exists from German TV, and
Kaye is masterful, particularly as his playing has to cover the studio-created

transitions present in the original. Like many, I wish the band had played this track live more often, although they did hint at it during the version of 'The Fish' played on the 1978/ 1979 *Tormato* tour.

Related tracks
'Everydays' (Stephen Stills)
This Stephen Stills song was a live favourite and it's not hard to see why. The track has a great sense of dynamics, with a perfect midsection to allow organ and guitar soloing. Of the two versions on the Rhino re-master, the so-called 'single version' is the stronger and longer, with great interplay between Banks and Kaye, and a keyboard run from Kaye that is almost Wakeman-like in its dexterity. The shorter version is also good – it has some great singing from Anderson, and Banks playfully throws a snatch of 'Jesu Joy Of Man's Desiring' into his solo.

'Dear Father' (Anderson, Squire)
Another pop song in the 'Looking Around' mould, the track languished as a *Time And A Word* era B-side, although both the versions on the Rhino re-master are perfectly decent, with version two a little more polished than version one, although its predecessor does have a great deal of energy. Most Yes fans were introduced to this song when it was included on the Yesterdays compilation, released in 1974.

'Something's Coming' (Leonard Bernstein, Stephen Sondheim)
The band's expansive arrangement for this classic song from West Side Story was the most significant piece in the Yes repertoire circa early 1969 to fail to make it onto a finished album. However, as the two versions on the Rhino re-master show, it certainly deserves some sort of airing. It shows off everything that was good – and not quite so good – about this early version of the band. They certainly knew how to fashion an arrangement and the backing vocals are exceptional in both versions. The main – later – recording is the tighter of the two, although Banks' playful addition of 'Troika' by Prokofiev is perhaps a touch too knowing – I prefer his playing on the earlier, rawer version.

Time and a Word (1970)

Personnel:
Jon Anderson: vocals
Chris Squire: bass, vocals
Peter Banks: guitar, vocals
Bill Bruford: drums
Tony Kaye: organ, piano
David Foster: backing vocals, acoustic guitar
Produced at Advision, December 1969 – February 1970, Produced by Tony
Colton, Orchestral Arrangements Tony Cox, Engineer Eddie Offord
UK release date: July 1970, US release date: November 1970
Highest Chart Places: UK: 45, USA: none
Running time: 39:35

What to do? Despite their growing reputation as a live unit, the response to
the band's debut album had been a disappointment to everyone. While it
would be an exaggeration to suggest that panic had set in, there was clearly
a feeling that something needed to change. What the band might have done
was trust in their material and their arrangements since there is little doubt
that the songs on *Time and a Word* are in improvement on the previous
album. Two things happened that were to change everything, both seemingly
instigated by Jon Anderson. Firstly, the band decided to use an orchestra
to augment the arrangements. This was quite fashionable at the time, as
both The Nice and Deep Purple had attempted this reasonably successfully.
Secondly, Anderson brought in his friend Tony Colton to produce. Colton was
the singer of the recently-formed Head, Hands and Feet (with Albert Lee on
guitar) and had ambitions in the area of production.

While the album sounds markedly better than its predecessor – probably
due to the skilled work of a young engineer called Eddie Offord, to become
an important figure on later albums – the orchestral arrangements do
'squeeze' the organ and guitar parts. Yet it is Banks that suffers most. The
guitarist argued that Colton's love of blues-based playing did not suit Banks'
style, bringing him into conflict with the producer and unsettling the band,
and while there is still plenty of guitar to be found on the album, it is not as
prominent as it might have been. By contrast, Kaye seems to find the space
he needs to make a good impression, a remarkable achievement since the
'job' of a keyboard player in rock music is often to provide orchestral colour.

Otherwise, the structure of the album is similar to the first, with two cover
versions and six originals which mix styles from pop to near symphonic rock.
The material is more confident, certainly, and in 'Astral Traveller', the band
had perhaps found a direction which might work for them playing original
material going forward. However, the orchestra, an interesting gimmick
though it was, holds the band back from a sound that was developing and
improving anyway. Two concerts at the Queen Elizabeth Hall with and a

twenty-piece orchestra (twenty 'pieces' is not a lot) was a partial success at best, and by the late spring of 1970, Banks was out.

'No Opportunity Necessary, No Experience Needed' (Richie Havens)
The orchestra works well on this opening piece which mixes a fairly straight rendition of a Richie Havens song – albeit with the usual Yes-style harmonies and some powerful organ – with, well, the theme to the well-known Western film, *The Big Country* (whose author, rather unfortunately, receives no writing credit). It works because the orchestra only interjects during the Western-style section, leaving the band to storm through the main song unencumbered.

Banks is well featured and even throws in a section from 'The Big Country' theme himself. A rawer mix can also be found on the Rhino re-master. It has some of Banks' guitar parts – missing from the final mix – re-inserted.

Steve Howe reveres the band prior to his arrival, and as a result, this song has made appearances in 2022 live sets.

'Then' (Anderson)
This is a very strong song written by Anderson – one of the pieces from the album that has stood the test of time. Again, the orchestra – swapping 'licks' with Kaye's organ – works nicely on the verses, but embellishes unnecessarily on the chorus. Kaye is indeed the star here – his solos in the instrumental section are excellent, as is Squire's bass work, while Banks is relegated to rhythm. The breakdown to the quiet section towards the end of the track is nicely done, as is the final 'big band' jazz outro. Nonetheless, this is one of those pieces that didn't really need the orchestra, as the live versions on the Banks-compiled *Something's Coming* album of BBC sessions illustrate.

'Everydays' (Stephen Stills)
The same can be said of this – the third attempt to record this Stephen Stills song after two versions during the time of the first album. While the piece keeps the bare bones of the arrangement – with Banks' guitar prominent – the orchestral shimmers are completely unnecessary, and we are left longing for one of the versions recorded earlier.

'Sweet Dreams' (Anderson, David Foster)
This was the big single from the album – significantly, recorded without orchestra – and it is rather marvellous. It's straight, catchy pop with a lovely arrangement. Of all the songs from the album, except the title track, this song has had one of the longest live. It was played occasionally by the Moraz-era band, and also in almost every show on the 2004 world tour. The track was co-written with Anderson's band-mate from The Warriors, David Foster, who went on to form Badger with Tony Kaye. A slightly longer version – with a lot more Banks and a longer outro – can be heard on the Rhino re-master.

'The Prophet' (Anderson, Squire)

A huge neo-classical Hammond introduction from Kaye heralds the return of the orchestra and this splendid mini-epic, with hints of Eastern promise. Banks contributes a lovely, jazzy guitar solo and the song itself, when it arrives, is wonderful, with the orchestra once again providing tasteful embellishment rather than dominating, as it tends to do elsewhere on the album. It's a shame that this piece didn't linger longer in the live set, although Anderson did sing a snatch of it during his Yes medley on his solo *Song Of Seven* tour.

'Clear Days' (Anderson)

This is fragile, pleasant, yet forgettable stuff. Anderson sings a cloyingly-romantic tune with a somewhat over-arranged string quartet and (presumably) Kaye's piano. The ending is better than the song.

'Astral Traveller' (Anderson)

Tonally, this great piece is akin to 'Then', but without the orchestra, allowing the entire band – with both Kaye and Banks doing some great work in neo-classical style – to really let rip. This is the piece that heralds *The Yes Album* to the greatest extent, with Banks experimenting with some different textures and tones in the same way that Howe would do a year later. It's a terrific piece of tuneful, superbly arranged progressive rock, rendered somewhat more '1960s' by the odd effect on the vocals and the overall production quality.

'Time And A Word' (Anderson, Foster)

The title track has been rendered ... er... 'timeless' partly because of its lovely melody and universal sentiment, but also because of Anderson's habit of dusting it off on a regular basis. It was played live on the 1978-79 tour as part of the 'Big Medley' and also in the 1996 *Keys To Ascension* shows, while Anderson included it in his solo medley on the Anderson, Bruford, Wakeman, Howe tour. The Jon Davidson lineup has even played it on occasion to represent the Banks era of the band, even though Banks himself disliked the song. It is a nice tune, although not particularly 'Yes', and suffers from a scratchy guitar introduction, supposedly played by Dave Foster.

Related tracks

'Dear Father' (Anderson, Squire)

The final recording of the song, which appeared on the early German versions of the album in place of 'The Prophet' and on the B-side of 'Sweet Dreams', is a more sedate affair than the two recordings that had preceded it, with a rather stately orchestra high in the mix, but it's fine nonetheless. It first saw the light of day in this version on the *Yesterdays* compilation in 1975.

'For Everyone' (Anderson, Squire)
A live version of this song exists from a BBC live set, recorded in March 1970. It feels like a work in progress, with two sections that don't quite fit together. It is a nice Anderson song with a catchy organ riff from Kaye, followed by an early version of 'Disillusion', sung solo by Squire, later to appear as part of 'Starship Trooper'. As a way of demonstrating that *The Yes Album* wasn't created from scratch in that farmhouse in Devon, it is an interesting glimpse into the past.

The Yes Album (1971)

Personnel:

Jon Anderson: vocals, percussion

Chris Squire: bass guitar, vocals

Steve Howe: electric and acoustic guitars, Vachalia, vocals

Tony Kaye: piano, organ, Moog

Bill Bruford: drums, percussion

Produced at Advision, Autumn 1970 by Yes and Eddie Offord

Released date: February 1971

Highest chart places: UK: 4, USA: 40. Running time: 41:32

The band suffered its first real crisis in the spring of 1970 with the dismissal of Peter Banks. Having fallen out with producer Tony Colton during the *Time and A Word* sessions, he was eventually fired by Anderson and Squire, an event which left him deeply wounded and which would overshadow the rest of his career. His replacement was Steve Howe, who seems to have been talent-spotted by Squire and Anderson, and it isn't hard to see why. Jazzy and loose, Peter Banks' style fitted the band of the first couple of albums perfectly, with its post-psychedelic, proto-progressive hybrid. However, Howe brought something very different to the band. As well as being an unusual and inventive lead player in the rock idiom, he was well-versed in a variety of styles, including the clean jazz of Wes Montgomery and the finger-picking style of Chet Atkins. He was also heavily influenced by classical and flamenco guitar. Although he was always willing to use different sounds and textures – he was an early pioneer of the use of the pedal steel and electric sitar in rock music – his early reliance on his Gibson 175-D hollow-bodied electric gave him a rock sound like no other guitarist.

Howe came in at an awkward time for the band and found himself initially promoting the *Time and a Word* album, even appearing on the American cover and some whacky promotional videos. The band mixed up gigs during the Summer of 1970 with intense rehearsals. But when the album was finally released in the UK, it became very clear that this second album was not to be the success they had hoped for, and during their subsequent rehearsals, they were very aware that they were in the 'last chance saloon' with their label Atlantic. Indeed, it appears that they were to be dropped but that their main supporter at the label, Phil Carson, bailed them out at the last minute.

Yes fans still speculate about what might have happened in that house in Devon while they worked on the new material. Was it desperation that pushed them to the new level they reached in the composition of this album, or was it that extra spark of energy that Howe provided? What emerged from their time in the West Country was such a great leap forward – an evolutionary jump to rival the Cambrian explosion – that, as a Yes fan, it almost boggles the mind. All of the album – with the exception of 'A Venture' – remains in the band's main repertoire to this day. The tracks remain band

and fan favourites, endlessly re-interpreted (with respect, of course) by whichever incarnation happens to exist at the time.

Three things seem to have happened when looking at the album as a whole:

Firstly, the band were hugely confident as a unit, some of which will have been down to natural progression resulting from the two years they had been playing together. However, they also had the foresight not to rely on cover versions to fill out albums as they had previously. They were determined to forge their own path in whatever direction it took them.

Secondly, there is little doubt that Steve Howe's presence gave them a genuine shot in the arm. Peter Banks was a talented musician, but Howe came in brimming with ideas and also possibilities. Much mimicked and copied in later years, it would simply not have been possible for another musician to come in with such a huge breadth of influences. Rock musicians these days have so much more actual rock history to fall back on. Howe drew inspiration from Jimi Hendrix and Eric Clapton, of course, but he was also listening to the blues, to jazz and bluegrass and even classical guitar music. He had so much more colour to draw upon than most rock guitarists.

Finally, when we listen to The Yes Album now, we do not hear the 1960s, we hear modernity. The first two albums were well recorded for their time; indeed, the band recorded *The Yes Album* at the same studio (Advision) as *Time and a Word* and with the same engineer in Eddie Offord. Yet The Yes Album sounds completely different. It has an almost antiseptic clarity to it. Gone is that bass-y boom that characterised much of the recording of the late 1960s. Instead, we have an album where each instrument stands alone in the mix, clear and intimate. The vocals, for instance, are recorded with far less reverb than previously, and sit high in the mix. Tony Kaye's organ is also nakedly prominent. In the course of little more than six months, the band had left the 1960s and joined 'the modern era'.

Released in February 1971, the album was a commercial success in the UK, reaching number four and a minor one in the USA. Chris Squire often suggested that the album charted so well due to a postal strike in Britain during early 1971 which meant that when the album was first released, chart returns could only be counted from London-based record stores, where Yes had a strong following. But then again, most rock bands need a little dose of luck occasionally, so it is hard to begrudge them a little accidental leg up, whether there is truth in the story or not.

The Yes Album is innovative and groundbreaking, and yet I rarely play it. While I recognise how hugely important it is in the Yes story, the pieces on it have had so many superb live interpretations over the years that the originals now seem a little naive. Additionally, so deft is the exuberant playing of Howe throughout the album that Tony Kaye – often a dexterous player in the past– seems a little out of place, even obvious at times, particularly with his organ arrangements. It is not hard to see why this was the next area that the band felt they needed improvement in. Although now seen as a ground-breaking progressive rock record, playing it again, it is definitely a transitional album. While he has since become a poster boy for avoiding cliché in guitar playing, on his first album in the band Steve Howe actually plays a fair amount of blues- based licks, and had Kaye stayed it is quite possible that the band might have developed into a harder-edged outfit. But in the end, with the arrival of Rick Wakeman, a more progressive path was chosen.

'Yours Is No Disgrace' (Anderson, Squire, Howe, Kaye, Bruford)
As a statement of intent, it doesn't get much better than this. The 'new' Yes is presented here, fully-formed and in all its glory in a song that is clearly – and famously – about the Vietnam war. Meanwhile, the sound is pristine – dry, almost. Each instrument can be heard, crystal clear without being buried in unnecessary reverb. The initial unison riff gives way to big Hammond organ chords and the first vocal section. One of the important features of this track is the lack of a 'lead' vocal for most of the song – it's a three-part harmony for almost all the verses, with Howe soloing between phrases. This is terrific, stirring stuff, with Howe and also Bruford on fire. This section also features the first use of a Moog Synthesiser on a Yes album – playing the melody line. The next section is the same vocal line, but this time – brilliantly – sung over a simple, mostly ascending bass line. Then we're back into a repeat of the opening salvo before an extended instrumental section, beginning with some percussive guitar work before a lengthy and innovative solo from Howe – relatively short here, but extended for several minutes at live shows. In fact, it's not a single solo, but two overlapping ones, with very different voicings. Then, at last, there's a lead vocal – Anderson singing over a simple bass and acoustic guitar pattern before a return to the main verse played by the full band to a close.

'Yours Is No Disgrace' is nine minutes and 40 seconds of real innovation. The band had never tried anything as bold in its construction as this, and it immediately demonstrated that Howe was a genuine and prodigious talent. With Eddie Offord making each instrument sound astonishing, it is no wonder that the piece has lasted so well, regularly part of the live set almost 50 years later. As the *Yessongs* version shows, the piece became a jumping-off point for Howe to improvise boldly. Indeed, the version on that live album is interesting as it's clear that Howe's solo could go on for as long as he wanted, and you can hear him trying things – not all of which come off – but it must have been thrilling to be in the room as he improvised.

'Clap' (Howe)
Forever known as 'The Clap' due to Anderson's mischievous mistitling on this live recording, this remains Howe's most famous solo guitar piece. It has been performed thousands of times at live performances, sometimes played dead straight or often rearranged with other acoustic pieces. It remains the centrepiece of Howe's acoustic set – usually two tracks long – to this day.

It's a lovely Chet Atkins-influenced piece with hints of 'Classical Gas' (by US guitarist Mason Williams) in its chord structure. However, it's hard to believe it is worthy of so much attention; after all, it's a splendid – but hardly consequential – little piece. It shows what resonance this album has with Yes's fan base that even a 'throw away' track like this can resonate down through the decades.

A studio version of it can be found on the Steven Wilson remix, which also includes a section from 'Mood For A Day'. It's not as good – there are a couple of missed notes and a rather buzzy string. The live version was recorded at the Lyceum in London on 17 July 1970 – one of Howe's first gigs with the band.

'Starship Trooper (Life Seeker / Disillusion / Würm)' (Anderson, Squire, Howe)

While 'Yours Is No Disgrace' was almost perfect 'right out of the box', 'Starship Trooper' feels a touch sterile in its studio incarnation; so many wonderful live versions have there been over the years. Rather than the sophisticated layering of sections in the opening track, here we have three parts – one after the other – but the pieces still work together, and the band – in almost 50 years – have never really altered them in the thousands of live arrangements .

The opening section – 'Life Seeker' – written by Anderson, is something he might have written during the *Time And A Word* era, but here the arrangement is much more confident and bold. Again, Kaye plays some Moog for colour, and his Hammond and Howe's guitar complement each other nicely. Howe's frantically-picked acoustic guitar introduces 'Disillusion', written by Squire, originally to be found as part of a song 'For Everyone', a piece from the Banks era that was later abandoned. There's a live version on the *Beyond And Before* compilation of live and session tracks compiled by Banks in 1997. In that version, it's sung by Squire. However, on *The Yes Album,* it's sung by Anderson with a harmony vocal from Squire. The close harmony vocal section reintroduces 'Life Seeker' briefly, before the 'Würm' section – basically, a three-chord sequence repeated with embellishments by the band, a gradual increase in activity from Bruford and a guitar solo – again, a duet, on both sides of the stereo – from Howe to the fade out.

Kaye's own organ embellishments in the 'Würm' section on the album version seem tame, given what we now know about subsequent live versions, but presumably, it was what he was asked to do at the time, with the limelight going – again – to Howe. All the 'markers' we know from live renditions are there on the studio version, including Squire's dainty bass figure just before the guitar solos. The band will have known at the time that the potential for this track as a live piece was huge, but the nine-minute song has grown to almost fifteen minutes in some cases. Given its usual place as a encore, there have been many arrangement embellishments over the years, including two fabulous Wakeman Minimoog solos on the spectacular *Tormato* tour version, still only available as a bootleg. Indeed, the 'Würm' section can include bass, synthesiser or organ solos before the main guitar solo, or even a duet between Moog and guitar. Although not used as often as 'Roundabout' as a final encore, it never fails to bring the house down.

'I've Seen All Good People (Your Move / All Good People)'
(Anderson, Squire)
If side one of the album defined Yes's new style of progressive rock, then the first track on side two was to show off a new-found confidence in songwriting – and just a hint of the good-time rock that, as a band, they were moving away from. Again, this famous track has been played at the vast majority of live performances since.

'Your Move' is possibly Anderson's finest 'conventional' song, but it could only have been written in the era it was – as the optimism of the 1960s gave way to the rather more cynical 1970s. Its chess metaphor for human relationships is nicely done – it could easily have been overbearing – and the backing vocals are beautifully arranged. So too, are Colin Goldring's recorders – a rare example of a guest musician playing on a Yes album in the early years. Howe plays the Portuguese twelve-stringed instrument Vachalia on this track, as he was also to do on 'Wonderous Stories' on *Going For The One*. The insertion of John Lennon's famous 'All We Are Saying Is Give Peace A Chance' line as a counterpoint to the main melody could only have worked in the early 1970s. Any time after the *Fragile* era, and it might have seemed trite. The final surge at the end of the track is followed by an uncomfortable silence in this studio version, leading into the 'All Good People' section written by Squire.

This is pretty much blues rock – a repetitive vocal line over a simple chord progression, with Howe soloing on his trusty Gibson ES-175. To be honest, while this section works really well as a clap/dance-along piece at live shows, here it feels sterile and a little uncomfortable; well played though it is.

'A Venture' (Anderson)
This brief track has always been considered the other 'throw away' piece on the album, but it works very nicely as a palette cleanser before the big finish of 'Perpetual Change'. Tonally, it is not dissimilar to the much better-known 'Long Distance Runaround', with a jaunty, off-beat arrangement, some nice (if unspectacular) piano work from Kaye and some very good lead guitar work from Howe. The Steven Wilson remix has an extended version of the track which is excellent. In it, the song continues into a rather decent jam which would have worked well on the album, but the fade-out is understandable given the time constraints of a side of vinyl. The band had bigger fish to fry!

The song has rarely been played live – although Howe has always expressed a liking for it, and even played it during his guest appearances

with the Yes tribute band, Fragile. It was, of course, played when the band
played the whole album in their 'single album' shows.

'Perpetual Change' (Anderson, Squire)

And so to the big finish. 'Perpetual Change' straddles the line between
possible directions for the band – between a classic/hard rock path and
something a little more neo-classical. It begins with a unison riff played by
guitar and piano, and Howe's playing, again, is more blues-orientated than it
was to be on later albums. The softer main verse has some good piano work
from Kaye, with Howe playing harmonics. Strangely enough, Kaye's piano
playing is more impressive than his organ work on The Yes Album and the
'You'll See Perpetual Change' 'hook' has a real feeling of rhythm and blues
about it. There's a sudden segue into a much jazzier passage, featuring a
hugely impressive and fluid solo from Howe, before the uber-prog of the
quirky guitar/organ/bass/drums figure, gradually moving to the left of the
stereo – before real innovation another full band arrangement seeps in from
the right playing something completely different until meeting in the middle
on a swirl of Moog synthesiser, a return to the main chorus and a big finish
to the final fade out.

The section where there are 'two bands' playing presents a challenge to
the band when arranging as a live piece, but they accomplished it and once
again, it has become a staple – if not exactly a constant – of the live set. It is
sometimes played as an opener, and like 'Yours Is No Disgrace' can – and has
– been extended to allow longer solos.

Fragile (1971)

Personnel:
Jon Anderson: vocals
Bill Bruford: drums and percussion
Steve Howe: electric and acoustic guitars, vocals
Chris Squire: bass guitars and vocals
Rick Wakeman: organ, grand piano, electric piano, harpsichord, mellotron,
synthesiser
Produced at Advision, September 1971 by Yes and Eddie Offord. Engineered by
Eddie Offord, assisted by Gary Martin
UK Release date: December 1971. US release date: January 1972
Highest chart places: UK: 7, USA: 4
Running time: 41:10

Fragile saw another lineup change – and a crucial one at that – with Tony
Kaye replaced by Strawbs (and session) keyboard player Rick Wakeman.
Kaye had begun to sound out of his depth on *The Yes Album*, and while
it does actually contain a fair amount of synthesiser, his performance was
still largely organ-based. There is also a suggestion of a personality clash
between the hard-partying Kaye and the more reserved Howe, but in the
end, Squire and Anderson wanted something a little more orchestral, and
Wakeman – who had already played Mellotron on David Bowie's 'Space
Oddity' as early as 1969 – seemed perfect. His virtuosity was somewhat
misplaced and underutilised in his current band, The Strawbs – as a listen to
their excellent *Just a Collection of Antiques and Curios* live album testifies.
   The new lineup began rehearsing immediately after Kaye's departure,
and worked up new material for an album which – label Atlantic and
the band hoped – would capitalise quickly on the considerable success
of *The Yes Album*. The material was very strong, but only one problem
remained. There wasn't enough of it. As a result, each member of the group
contributed a solo track with varying degrees of success. Howe's 'Mood
for a Day', for instance, is a delightful classical piece – in contrast to the
Country pickin' of 'Clap', while Squire and Anderson's pieces also have a
lot of charm. Wakeman's 'Cans and Brahams' is hampered by his contract
with A&M Records which prevented him from contributing a self-penned
piece, and Bruford's track feels a little pointless. However, the band-created
pieces are astonishing. In particular, Wakeman's parts on this (and *Close
to the Edge*) are his most imaginative and integrated contributions to the
Yes catalogue. Alongside his florid virtuosity and undoubted talents with
multiple keyboards, his classical training enhanced the band's ability to
transition between sections within a single track. All four of the full-band
pieces have remained in the band's live set – more on than off – since
the album was released. Yet the solo tracks blight the album just a little.
Another month spent on the record might have removed the need for these

pieces and produced the classic that was not to arrive for a few months with *Close to the Edge*.

This was the first Yes album to make use of the skills of Roger Dean, an elegant and amiable Englishman whose unique fantasy paintings have become so synonymous with the band's music. Note that the band's famous snake-like logo had not yet arrived – but the other-worldly nature of the artwork fitted perfectly with the ambiguous nature of Anderson's lyrics. The vinyl version of the album came complete with a gatefold sleeve and a booklet – reproduced in miniature in the 2016 Definitive Edition CD. Clearly, neither the band nor Atlantic were taking any chances.

'Roundabout' (Anderson, Howe)

This iconic rocker remains the perfect calling card to the 'classic' version of the band. Howe's classical guitar introduction leads into the main song, which emphasises Squire's mobile bass and Wakeman's terrific organ arpeggios. It is possible to imagine Kaye playing this – but not with quite such effortless fluidity. Bruford's cymbal work – as usual – is first-rate on the middle section, which also includes some unusual organ chords that Kaye could not have contributed, plus the first of the characteristic vocal harmony sections so beloved of the band. Listen out, too, for the casual virtuosity of Wakeman's playing – low in the mix – over the acoustic guitar reprise before the first Mellotron appearance on a Yes album, and that great organ/guitar dual before the final reprise of the main theme. The track lays out the sound palette of the album both instrumentally and tonally. The 1960s have gone entirely by this point and any of the clean sterility that might have – slightly – blighted *The Yes Album* has been replaced by a warm, natural and – it has to be said – even more modern sound. If you are reading this, Eddie Offord, take a bow.

This most perfect of up-tempo Yes pieces has developed a life of its own, of course. An edited version of the song was a big – and unexpected – hit single in the USA, which – in turn – has led to it being played as an encore in almost every Yes show since. Sometimes – particularly when there is another guitarist alongside Howe (eg. Trevor Rabin or Billy Sherwood) playing in the band, a full version has been performed with Howe playing acoustic for the first couple of minutes of the track. At other times, various edits have been used – usually to preserve that full-tilt 'encore' vibe. On the 2004 world tour, the song was relegated to the acoustic section and played – entertainingly – as a shuffle. There are various alternative versions on the 2003 Rhino re-master and 2016 Definitive Edition (including the US single edit, which I had never heard before), and countless live versions, but the original on *Fragile* still takes some beating.

'Cans and Brahms' (Brahms Arr: Wakeman)

This is a slight piece – albeit a pleasant listen – and had it not been placed on such a famous album, it would never have warranted the attention it still gets to this day. Indeed, it has a bit of a 'Switched on Bach' feel to it, which may be intentional. However, as a calling card for Wakeman's ability, it does say a couple of things. Firstly: 'The classics are important to me' and secondly: 'look at how many keyboards I have'. Both these may seem obvious to us 50-plus years on, but given that most keyboard players were still rhythm and blues organists, it sends an important message to the Yes-buying public. When the band toured playing *Fragile* in its entirety in 2015, the track – played by Geoff Downes – seemed completely pointless.

'We Have Heaven' (Anderson)

'Tell the Moondog, tell the March hare'. Originally planned as an *a capella* piece, this Anderson solo track has a bit more about it than Wakeman's, with Anderson building up layered vocals over a very basic acoustic guitar, bass and drums backing. A longer version and an *a capella* mix can be found on the Steven Wilson Definitive Version Blu-ray. The song – like Wakeman's track, rather short – foreshadows Anderson's great solo album *Olias of Sunhillow* in 1976 with its joyous tone and beautifully-crafted backing vocals. Footsteps – panning nicely over the stereo – lead into the next piece, which is ...

'South Side of the Sky' (Anderson, Squire)

This full-band track is the first to use strong non-musical atmospherics on a Yes album, with rolls of thunder and swirls of wind introducing us to another rocker with Howe soloing hard and Anderson's double-tracked vocals wailing over a complex and powerful riff played by guitar, bass and organ in unison at times. After this hard-rocking section, the piece takes an unexpected turn with its neo-classical piano solo – again, the first of its type on a Yes album – and the following vocal section with Chris Squire dominant (rather than Anderson) and guitar almost completely absent. This is wonderfully done and lifts the track to something very special. Bruford gets the chance to use his jazz chops here, before a reprise of the hard rock section and a further swirl of wind close the track and, indeed, the first side of the album. There's a fantastic feeling of 'space' on this track. I love, for instance, the way that the final low piano note of Wakeman's solo section is allowed to resonate and swirl across the stereo before the next section. It's spectacular and confident stuff.

This great track was tried out as a live piece on the *Fragile* Tour but dropped quickly, as it didn't seem to gel. It may simply have been that the technology – particularly the live sonic reproduction of the grand piano, so critical to the piece – just did not work at the time. However, it was attempted successfully in 2003, when digital samples had made reproduction of a grand piano in a live rock setting much easier, and seemed to work so well it has been part of many live sets since. Played by the band of 2003-4, which included Howe and Wakeman, it was extended to include a thrilling guitar / Minimoog duel.

'Five per cent for nothing' (Bruford)

Bruford's 35-second instrumental track – played by the whole band – is somewhat throwaway due to its brevity. Seeing the band – in late middle age having to play this piece in a live setting due to a commitment to playing the complete album is a little silly. The title refers to the deal that Roy Flynn – the band's first manager – negotiated on his way out. Bruford has more recently admitted that his somewhat acerbic song title was a little unkind in retrospect.

'Long Distance Runaround' (Anderson)

Considering its relative fame in the catalogue, this lively but short piece feels rather slight in the cold light of day. Indeed, as a live track, it has tended to work as a full-band introduction to the same piece as it does on the album, Chris Squire's solo track 'The Fish'. It remains good fun, though, an early example of the way that Howe and Wakeman could feature in a track without getting in each other's way, usually playing in harmony – Howe on electric guitar, Wakeman on electric piano, then acoustic piano for the verses. Squire's wandering bass and Bruford's inventive snare work are both excellent, creating a stabbing arrangement to complement Anderson's tuneful song melody.

'The Fish (Schindleria Praematurus)' (Squire)

Often misrepresented as a bass solo, probably due to its use as a stepping-off point for a solo in live concerts, this inventive piece – mainly created by overdubbed bass guitars – actually includes some nice electric guitar and mallet percussion interjections, as well as the repeated vocal refrain just before the fade out. Unlike some of the live solos it inspired, the track also gets to the point quite quickly. Overall, it's an inventive use of the instrument and does bear repeated listening, unlike Bruford and Wakeman's solo pieces on this same album.

'Mood for a Day' (Howe)

Howe's classical guitar track really is a solo piece, showing off his growing maturity as a player and composer. The performance is not perfect, but it is spontaneous and dynamic, beautifully recorded with great warmth. Only 'Clap' retains more resonance with Yes fans, although 'Mood For A Day' is played in a live setting much less regularly.

'Heart of the Sunrise' (Anderson, Squire, Bruford)

Despite the great pieces that Yes had already committed to vinyl – not least 'Roundabout' which opens this album – 'Heart of the Sunrise' feels, to me, like the first true Yes masterpiece. It is the first true representation of what the mature Yes would be capable of. It is a seemingly effortless combination of virtuosity, extreme dynamics and structure over its eleven or so minutes.

The opening riff – carried by guitar and organ – is punctuated by a weird organ texture, in itself a masterstroke of arrangement, before the famous bass section, which builds in intensity due to the ascending Mellotron chords, Bruford's masterful drumming and the re-introduction, firstly via the guitar, of the main riff. There's nothing particularly complex about Squire's playing here, he's varying a simple riff, yet it's the building on tension that works so well.

The song then breaks down to the first vocal section – the band is tentative at first, before introducing themes that will appear in more powerful form later in the song, but here delicately played. Listen to the subtle keyboards in this section – a touch of Moog here, a snatch of piano there, and then 'sharp, distance' – brings us to the first peak. The next instrumental section combines the main riff with a counterbalancing, staccato section with Moog again dominant. The effortless way that Squire and Bruford switch between these two repeating sections is remarkable. Next, we are into the piano-led section – 'straight light moving and removing' – this is a new riff entirely, taken up by the whole band with Anderson now double-tracked and Wakeman switching between piano and organ, building to the final Mellotron swirl, and the powerful, triumphant final vocal section 'love comes to you, then after'. To a sixteen-year-old hearing this for the first time in 1978, this was life-changing music. It still sends shivers down my spine now. The piece ends playfully with an opening door and a return to 'We Have Heaven' – as if it continues forever in a room somewhere. You just need to open the right door ...

'Heart Of The Sunrise' has, of course, been played live many times over the years, usually in an arrangement close to the original. As a mid-set show-stopper, it is only challenged by 'And You And I'.

Related tracks
'Show Me' (Anderson)
I am placing this track here as – according to Anderson's introduction to the song on the New Director's Cut DVD – he found the song on an old cassette from this era. It is a sweet, folky ditty that was played on the 2003-4 tours, so can only be found on the *Songs from Tsongas* live CD set, as an interlude on the 2003 tour (with Wakeman) and in the acoustic set in 2004 (and on the *Yes Acoustic* DVD) with a slightly different arrangement.

'America' (Simon)
A remnant from the covers band of 1968-69, the group first recorded a shorter version of their – somewhat expansive – ten-minute arrangement of this Simon and Garfunkel song with Kaye on organ before definitively re-recording it – with Wakeman on organ, Mellotron and electric piano – for an Atlantic Records compilation in 1971. An earlier, inferior live version can be found on the *Word is Live* album. The final, guitar-dominated version from 1971 features only parts of the original Paul Simon song, and somewhat

sidelines Wakeman, who, according to Howe, wasn't especially interested in the recording, although as a backup player his contributions are still good. It has reared its head occasionally in live sets over the years – most notably in 1996 for *The Keys To Ascension* live shows and in 2008 on the *Open Your Eyes* Tour.

'All Fighters Past' (precise authorship unknown)
Discovered by remix maestro Steven Wilson on the master tapes from this era and to be found only on the Blu-ray in his reissue of *Fragile*, this full-band piece was understandably dropped, with both tune and lyrics recycled for 'The Revealing Science of God' two years later.

Close to the Edge (1972)

Personnel:
Jon Anderson: vocals
Bill Bruford: percussion
Steve Howe: guitars, vocals
Chris Squire: bass, vocals
Rick Wakeman: keyboards
Produced at Advision, February to June 1972 by Yes and Eddie Offord. Tapes:
Mike Dunne. Co-ordinator: Brian Lane
Released: September 1972
Highest chart places: UK: 4, USA: 5
Running time: 37:51

And so to *Close To The Edge*. This astonishing piece of work is one of the most celebrated albums of the progressive rock era, and one wonders what to say about an album that has been so talked about, so analysed and so loved. The album has been discussed a great deal over the years. Musicologist Edward Macan discussed the side-long title track in detail in his *Rocking the Classics* book, while journalist Will Romano dedicated an entire book to the album in 2017 with his *Close To The Edge: How Yes's Masterpiece Defined Progressive Rock*. What needs to be said? Well, let me give it a go ...

Fragile, for all its success, was based around a relatively small amount of band-created material, essentially three long pieces in 'Roundabout', 'South Side of the Sky' and 'Heart of the Sunrise'. The album had been produced in something of a hurry to meet demand, especially in the UK, but had gone on to reach markets the band could only have dreamed about. Now the time had come to work on a new band album. The main bulk of the new record was rehearsed in the spring of 1972 and then recorded in June, although it is clear that by the time they went into Advison with Eddie Offord, they were still writing material, leading to a somewhat tortuous and argumentative process. In his autobiography, Bill Bruford refers to the band at the time as being 'painfully democratic', with every decision during the making of the album argued over endlessly. The band had complete creative freedom, and they exercised it.

Every bar and every instrumental choice was agonised over endlessly. Bruford hated the process, but with Yes in one of those rare states where every member had equal status, this is how the band operated. On this occasion, whether by fluke, genius or a combination of both, it worked. The material was rehearsed during the spring of 1972 at the Una Billings School of Dance in Shepherd's Bush before transitioning into recording time at Advision in June. It has often been noted that on the back cover of the album, there are six photographs, all of equal size and status. There is one shot of each member of the band, plus Eddie Offord. The message is clear. 'There are six of us in the band now.'

Close to the Edge is, arguably, progressive rock's defining statement. It is 38 minutes of power, tenderness and passion. It is, by turns, atonal and supremely melodic, it is powerful and gentle, both intensely meaningful and, at the same time, completely and dazzlingly meaningless. It contains surprises and it even contains some mistakes, but it contains not one second of filler. The music drips with atmosphere, which is achieved not just by the musicianship of the players but by clever transitions and uses of reverb, effects and microphone positioning. Furthermore, each musician is at the top of his game. The creativity on display is astonishing, yet the process was too much for Bruford, who moved on to join King Crimson shortly after the completion of the album.

'Close to the Edge (The Solid Time of Change / Total Mass Retain / I Get up, I Get Down / Seasons Of Man)' (Anderson, Howe)

Having mastered ten-minute pieces on the previous two albums, Yes decided to attempt a single, side-long piece of music, and right out of the traps, they nailed it. They were not the only band to consider this idea at the time; at the same time that Yes exited Una Billings School of Dance to go to Advsion, Genesis were setting up in the same location to rehearse *Foxtrot* which was to have its own side-long piece 'Suppers Ready'. Indeed, given the classical composers that the band – particularly Anderson – were listening to, like Sibelius, Mahler and Stravinsky, who often produced complex movements and suites that clocked in at around a side of vinyl, it must have seemed a natural – if ambitious – continuation of the band's growth.

From the start of the track, it is made very clear that we are entering a very special 'world'. A mixture of synthesiser birdsong and keyboard effects leads us into the opening section, perhaps the most controversial sequence on the album as it is quite atonal, with Howe's guitar soloing over a discordant, almost chaotic pattern, with Wakeman's organ part seemingly unrelated to what the rest of the band are playing, punctuated by Anderson's multi-tracked 'aaaahhhs'. As a solo section in the middle of a piece, this opening salvo would not be controversial, but as the opening of a track, it is provocative. Is it all going to be like this?

No, as it turns out, because, at three minutes, the opening section resolves itself with more massed voices, and segues into the superb main theme, played on guitar, which is then varied with a relatively conventional progressive arrangement with Wakeman continuing on organ. The first vocal section, 'A seasoned witch could call you...' begins, with Squire's bass swooping in and out and Howe accompanying on electric sitar. Cleverly, Anderson had been the only backing vocalist to that point, but at the 'chorus' – 'down at the edge, round by the corner' – we also hear Squire and Howe, before heading straight into a simpler section, with percussive keyboards, and a re-iteration of the chorus. 'Total Mass Retain' is largely a re-iteration of the first section, but Anderson's voice changes here – a touch more urgent

YES ... On Track

and presented with a touch less reverb. Squire and Bruford are astonishing – locked together but landing their blows in unexpected, almost random patterns. Wakeman punctuates the verses with alternate sections of Mellotron and Moog. After 'I get up, I get down', a key change heralds an instrumental section with bass and sitar playing one melody, while an organ plays a variation of the main theme.

It's all change for the third section, 'I Get up, I Get down'. No longer are we in a forest, we are now deep underground, the mood set by a Mellotron, drenched in reverb, some guitar low in the mix and bass Moog patterns. We hear drips of water, placing us in a huge cave, the band lost in its magnitude. This is resolved by a simple chord pattern, played on organ followed by two vocal melodies, the first 'in her white lace...' sung by Howe and Squire, and the counterpoint by Anderson of 'I get up, I get down..'. This is simply beautiful, a remarkable piece of construction, with Squire's backing vocals at their very best. The climax introduces Wakeman's massive-sounding church organ – recorded remotely at St.Giles-without-Cripplegate Church in London, and then spliced in by Offord – which, after a solo section, is then accompanied by another chorus of 'I get up, I get down' – Anderson alone this time. With the organ still playing, we build to a climax via a series of powerful Minimoog runs, and then three Moog 'chimes' doubled by percussion, and the band thumps back in, for the closing 'Seasons Of Man' section. Moog now plays a variation on the main theme, leading into 'that' famed Hammond organ solo. This is high-octane stuff, with the band's accompaniment daring and imaginative. Wakeman makes a couple of little mistakes in the solo – there's a tiny bum note at 15.51, for instance (have a listen) – but the take will have been used for its energy, no doubt. It is spine-tingling, air-keyboard-inducing stuff. The final section re-iterates the opening verses, but with Squire and Bruford varying their parts brilliantly before the final, climactic reprise of the chorus. Wakeman now plays Mellotron and piano rather than organ, and we fade away back into the chorus of birds, leaving the listener breathless.

Anderson and Howe's lyrics remain about as open to interpretation as any of Yes' pieces. We have many allusions to what may be the 'river of life' and also the change and evolution of mankind, but I will leave others to attempt better interpretations, as several have. What is most thrilling here is the way themes are introduced and endlessly varied in so many exciting ways. Wakeman's compositional training seems to have been important, glueing the arrangements together in a far more sophisticated way than the band had attempted before. It is eighteen minutes and 42 seconds long, and every second counts.

Although not as obvious a 'shoe-in' for the setlist as (say) 'And You And I' the band have played 'Close To The Edge' live hundreds of times over the years, and while several keyboard players have played it in addition to Wakeman – Moraz, Downs, Khoroshev and even session man Tom Brislin on

YES ... *On Track*

the Symphonic Tour, for instance – Howe has played the guitar on every live version to date. Unlike 'And You And I', it has never been played with Rabin in the band. As a closely arranged piece of music, there have been relatively few attempts to alter the instrumentation, although Alan White changed the drum part a fair amount when he first played it in 1972. Given that the church organ section could not be reproduced live until the 1990s, the band have always accentuated this section with percussion and bass to add drama. The organ solo is an opportunity for improvisation, but otherwise, the band have always stuck pretty close to the original recording, so there are many versions to choose from – of varying quality, tempo and recording skill, of course – but only differing slightly in it's basic arrangement.

'And You and I (Cord Of Life / Eclipse / The Preacher, The Teacher / Apocalypse)' (Anderson, Bruford, Howe, Squire)

After the intensity of the title track (or 'side one'), we mellow out for a while with this ten-minute masterpiece. 'And You And I' is one of only three pieces – 'Roundabout' and 'I've Seen All Good People' are the other two – deemed necessary to play at almost every live show. Howe plays a few harmonics, says 'ok' and we begin. This is a confident and intimate start, and worth noting. Many songs, throughout the ages, begin with a count in or studio chatter, but nobody does it quite like this.

It's a simple and effective opening, a little guitar figure – beautifully recorded (you can hear the natural reverb in the room) – before the gentle bass guitar and bass drum pulse brings in Howe's strummed riff; there's a triangle in there too, leading to Wakeman's iconic Minimoog solo which introduces Anderson's first vocal. Howe's guitar provides a counterpoint, followed by the full band, and the first statement of the 'chorus' such as it is, and a big build to the fantastic 'Eclipse' section, written by Bruford and Squire, but dominated by the superb combination of Mellotron and Moog playing in unison which delivers a huge emotional punch, augmented by Howe's guitar and Anderson's emotion-drenched lead vocal. We return to Howe's tentative twelve-string guitar figure, but this time it introduces a picked, country-style pattern in 'The Preacher, The Teacher' that suggests bluegrass, with Anderson's vocal delivered almost without reverb at all as a contrast to 'Eclipse', in what is the most 'conventional' section of the piece. Squire's bass re-enters with Howe now playing rhythm guitar and Wakeman vamping on Fender Rhodes piano before he then repeats the Moog line from earlier, this time extended into a solo, a final vocal section and a return to the 'Eclipse' theme – and a descending grand piano line, before the reiteration of the chorus and the faintest Moog note ascending in pitch into infinity...

To say this piece 'brings the house down' at live shows would be an understatement. Usually played mid-set (or occasionally before an interval), it is a cathartic moment for band and audience. However, it has had plenty of arrangement tweaks over the decades. In the years before acoustic instruments were usable in full-band settings, the band would open with the dramatic 'Eclipse' section before going straight into the initial strummed riff, usually played on a twelve-string electric. More recent performances, however, have returned to the gentle tone of the studio version. From early live performances onwards, Howe doubled Wakeman's keyboards in the 'Eclipse' section on pedal steel, with some embellishments, as this works better in a live setting. Squire added harmonica to the 'Preacher, Teacher' section, presumably to complement the country/bluegrass style. Trevor Rabin always plays his parts with great respect to Howe's originals when playing this piece.

'Siberian Khatru' (Anderson, Howe, Wakeman)
Given the intricacy and intensity of the first 29 minutes of the album, it is completely understandable that the band should want to rock out to close the record. But this is Yes – there is always a twist in the tale. Howe opens things up with an electric guitar figure followed by the main riff – played by Wakeman combining organ and Mellotron. Bruford's drumming seems simple, yet as usual, he places accents where you least expect them, leading into the main verse sung by a reverb-drenched Anderson, with Bruford's perky tambourine high in the mix and Wakeman playing some 'rock and roll' Hammond.

There's a nice moment of tension, with bass, guitar and snare only marking time, before the launch into the next verse. Howe's electric sitar figure leads into a completely unexpected harpsichord solo – beautifully played, too – accompanied, delightfully, just by Squire's bass. Next, Howe's pedal steel swaps solos with his own electric guitar. It is always a challenge to play these live, but Howe seems to be able to manage it, even in his 70s. Mellotron dominates the 'Hold Down The Window' section, an atmospheric interlude until we are back into the main theme again briefly, followed by the wonderfully tense and atmospheric 'outboard river' section, essentially a hugely evocative, yet also meaningless word list, with some inspired rhymes. This is clearly Anderson combining words for their sound rather than their meaning, but it works brilliantly. The section builds, with Mellotron and acoustic guitar dominant, soon joined by bass and Bruford's agile snare and with the tension broken, we are back into the main riff again and, after a final wordless vocal interlude, the track finishes on a terrific solo from Howe.

Another winning live track, 'Siberian Khatru', has most often been used as an opening piece – most notably on the *Close To The Edge* tour, the *Tormato* Tour and the *Tales* Tour. When not being used as an opener, it is usually not played at all. Although I am not a huge fan of Yes cover versions, I do love the Stanley Snail version on *Tales From Yesterday* – a Yes tribute album from 1996, which delivers a very faithful version of the track but wittily replaces the harpsichord solo with a section of 'The Sahara Of Snow Part One' from the Bruford album *One Of A Kind* – a personal favourite.

Tales From Topographic Oceans (1973)

Personnel:
Jon Anderson: vocals, guitar, percussion
Chris Squire: bass, vocals
Steve Howe: guitars, vocals
Alan White: drums, percussion, piano
Rick Wakeman: keyboards
Produced by Yes and Eddie Offord at Morgan Studios, London
Engineer: Nigel Luby. Co-ordination: Brian Lane
Released: December 1973
Highest chart places: UK: 1, USA: 6
Running time: 81:15

Most albums in the Yes catalogue cause some sort of debate between fans. Sometimes – as with *Close to the Edge* – the debate is simply about whether it is the greatest album they ever made, or whether it is simply in the top three. In other cases – like *Open Your Eyes*, for instance, the conversation is more about how poor it is. No album, however, has as much debate about its status within the band's discography as *Tales From Topographic Oceans*. For some – many, in fact – it is the crowning achievement of the band. For some, it is even the pinnacle of the progressive rock era. Yet for others – probably closer to a consensus – it is hugely flawed. To those, it contains some strong material, but spread too thinly, a prisoner of the album's overriding mission to present four tracks over four sides of a record for the first time. So, is it a bold masterpiece or a white elephant?

Let us first remember how far the band had come in little over four years. To date, each album had shown a huge leap in confidence, not to mention playing and compositional skill. Both Steve Howe and Rick Wakeman had added huge amounts to the band. Howe provided versatility and a daring sense of experimentation, while Wakeman added dexterity, a taste for technology and the ability to stitch pieces of music together so that they worked as a whole. But the five musicians also worked as an (albeit dysfunctional) unit. The arrival of Alan White – with his ferocious drumming but laid-back personality – possibly took a little of the combativeness out of the band, creatively.

Additionally, *Close to the Edge* had been created very much by the band as one rather tortuous unit, but it was Anderson and Howe that provided the lyrical and musical backbone that led to the creation of *Tales*. With two members taking the lead, the other three needed to be 'sold' the concept. It was not to be an easy task.

The two had conceived the album on tour during the spring of 1973 when Anderson read about the four Shastras in a footnote to the *Autobiography of a Yogi* by Paramahansa Yogananda, which had been given to him by Jamie Muir of King Crimson. In translating this into four long-form pieces, Anderson was also aspiring to symphonic works in the fashion of Sibelius or Mahler, a process begun on *Close To The Edge*.

This approach should be seen in the context of a natural – if ambitious – progression from that album. He and Steve Howe put together the lyrical and thematic basis of the album during that tour, finalising their ideas later that spring before beginning recording during the Summer and Autumn of 1973.

Not that Anderson didn't still have some strange ideas along the way. He wanted to record using a mobile studio in the countryside, leading to the crew putting bales of hay and cut-out cows in Morgan studios. He also asked for a tiled vocal booth to give him the sort of sound he got from singing in his bathroom. It didn't work. But by this time, the rest of the band had – somewhat reluctantly – agreed to Anderson and Howe's structure. Squire and Alan White – making his first appearance on a Yes studio album, let us not forget – bought into the project, making considerable contributions to the album. However, Wakeman was not enamoured of the material, and even though – as the Steven Wilson remix reveals – he is present for the entire album, his contributions are muted. Even on 'The Revealing Science of God', which includes his thrilling Minimoog solo towards the climax of the piece, some of his playing feels superficial. His sound palette, too, seems unimaginative. While there is some Hammond and piano dotted around, he mainly sticks to Minimoog and Mellotron, often played at the same time. Admittedly, these two instruments work very well together, but by contrast, Howe's palette is constantly – even thrillingly – inventive. In short, Wakeman is present, but he doesn't really contribute much creatively.

Tales is an elusive, frustrating album in many ways. Of course, going in with four twenty-minute pieces in mind from the start was arguably foolhardy and compared to the band at its most concise, almost every piece seems overextended, with sections regularly repeated. On the other hand, good ideas aren't developed enough, especially during 'The Remembering'. And yet, *Tales* remains my most-played Yes album. It has a tone unlike any other recording in the catalogue. I think the reason I enjoy it so much is that, unlike the slice of near-perfection that is *Close to the Edge*, its flaws are laid bare and very human. This time you could hear the band struggling a little, in a sense, trying to mould their ideas into four, neat, twenty-minute parcels but still producing something of sweeping invention in the end. What *Tales* does not deserve is the derision that was pointed at it for at least twenty years, not least from its keyboard player. It became one of the symbols, not just of the pomposity of progressive rock, but of the silliness of it. For many years, the two-word phrase 'prog rock' became one of derision, of a movement that should never have happened. Oh, how we fans suffered in those years!

But on the whole, *Tales* was considered a disappointment, even with friends of the band, like journalist Chris Welch, who generally thought that the band had gone too far in their ambition with this one.

Later in the decade, it was held up as an example of the excesses of the 'old guard' – the sort of bloated, excessive music that needed to be swept away. It's not hard to see why. The band exacerbated this by playing the album in its entirety on tour in the UK before it had been released. Indeed it was only in the spring of 1974 that they began to drop 'The Remembering from the set'. For Wakeman, the tour was to be his last work with Yes for two and a half years.

'The Revealing Science of God (Dance of the Dawn)' (Anderson, Howe, Squire, Wakeman, White)

Of the four 'movements' on *Tales*, 'The Revealing Science of God' and 'Ritual' are the band's most revived pieces over the years, the former being played at the *Keys to Ascension* shows in 1996 and also on the *Open Your Eyes* tour in 1998, plus the *Tales* tours in 2017 and 2018. There are many Yes tribute bands throughout the world, and 'The Revealing Science of God' is usually the piece from *Tales* they attempt first. Accessible and well-structured, it is the track that gets the balance between instrumentation just about right, with some superb contributions from Wakeman, particularly some terrific piano in the up-tempo 'Starlight, movement...' section, and of course, his astonishing Minimoog solo towards the end of the piece, surely his most thrilling contribution to any Yes album.

Yet in the 'perfect edit in my head', I think I would still lose three or four minutes. The track has a superb beginning – Anderson's chanted vocals and the gradual build of instruments leading into the opening Minimoog theme is exquisite. Some later versions of the track – most notably the Rhino remaster – have an ambient opening that was dropped for the final mix on the original version. This addition lessens the impact of the chanted beginning in my view, and was quite rightly removed for the 1973 double album set.

The track soon settles into a bit of a mid-tempo plod, however, with Howe soloing rather aimlessly, although the 'chorus' such as it is, is masterful, even catchy. Things improve during the powerful 'starlight, movement...' section, but this idea is dispensed with very quickly, replaced by another rather aimless section, although the 'rape the forest' vocal part with its dramatic Minimoog is excellent, followed by a return to the up-tempo section, and a terrifically inventive solo section from Howe. The 'young Christians' section – revived from the attempt to create a song from it in 1971 – is also wonderful, but the instrumental section that follows it takes rather too long to make its point, and Wakeman's solo – as we all know – is thrilling, made twice as good by the brilliance of the ensemble playing behind it and all the better for its brevity.

The track finishes with a restatement of the main theme – the sort of classically- inspired technique that the band were becoming masters at.

Despite my reservations, 'The Revealing Science of God' is a terrific start, made all the better by the fact that both Howe and Wakeman seem fully engaged and playing in harmony. Would it continue?

'The Remembering (High the Memory)' (Anderson, Howe, Squire, Wakeman, White)

The first of the two supposedly-problematic movements, 'The Remembering' is an odd, low-key piece of music. In many ways, it is lovely. It is tuneful, well played, particularly by Chris Squire, whose bass playing is a delicate delight throughout the track. The problem is that it doesn't really go anywhere, the arrangement is too linear, drifting along for a good nine minutes, with little Mellotron and Moog passages which seem to lack imagination in themselves. Only when the 'force between the mouth of freedom' section kicks in, with some acoustic textures at last, does the piece leap into life. The following 'Relayer' section is terrific, classic Yes at their best, with Wakeman's Moog to the fore, but it is over for the first time frustratingly quickly. The whole pattern repeats, ending again in trite atmospherics. The piece does end well with a little surge of excitement before petering out again. It is unclear whether Wakeman was not engaged enough to come up with something better here, or that the requirements of the piece did not suit his style. Probably both are true.

It is no wonder that this side was a challenging live proposition, both for the band and the audience. The frustrating thing is that this track has so much promise, some great melodies and some superb playing, as you might expect, but having played it dozens of times over 45 years, I still find it an annoying listening experience. It is a structural problem, I think, falling into repetition far too easily. Somewhere in there, there is a superb ten-minute piece trying to get out. 'The Remembering' was played on the *Tales* tour, although it was dropped in the second European leg in the early spring of 1974. It has never been revived in any way since, as far as I am aware.

I do understand the reverence some listeners have for it. It's a bit of a sonic *cul de sac* for Yes, perhaps hampered by its structure, which makes it very difficult to play live in its entirety as part of a rock show. But for many, it's the epitome of what makes this most immersive of albums the great work of art that is. Music is, after all, supremely subjective, and one man's frustration is another man's nirvana. Playing the piece again in 2023, I am struck by how magnificent the 'Relayer' section is. That it lies buried in a piece of music that is probably considered unplayable as a whole, is nothing short of tragic.

'The Ancient (Giants Under the Sun)' (Anderson, Howe, Squire, Wakeman, White)

Despite its difficult reputation, I like 'The Ancient'. I appreciate that little suggestion of jazz – the precursor of *Relayer* – and I admire the atmosphere that it creates. This is not just fashioned from the textures of Steve Howe's guitars, but from the invention in Alan White's percussion arrangements.

Unlike 'The Remembering', (arguably) there is real structure here. The opening instrumental section sets things up, before the Mellotron-led opening vocal passage and the tense instrumental section that follows it. So far, so good, and very Yes. In fact, there is nothing in the first eight minutes or so that is out of keeping with anything the band had produced on *Tales* or before. The 'trouble', if indeed trouble it is, comes roughly between the nine and twelve-minute marks, when the track veers off into free jazz, Frank Zappa territory. If this were King Crimson, this section would be hailed for the invention of Fripp's guitar work, but in Yes? Well, why not?

In context, this is barely three minutes before the piece resolves itself into the acoustic introduction to the famous ' Leaves of Green' section, with one of Steve Howe's best-loved classical guitar pieces and a charming, delicate vocal from Anderson. It seems to me that three minutes of rather 'wild' music in the middle of an otherwise challenging but relatively accessible piece has turned many listeners – and possibly a keyboard player – away from a track that they would otherwise find very rewarding.

'The Ancient' was played live on the. 1974 *Tales* tour but has not been played since. However, the 'Leaves of Green' section has appeared fairly regularly on setlists whenever Howe has been in the band. It was occasionally played, for instance, on the *Tormato* tour in 1978-1979 and on the 2017-2018 *Topographic* tours.

'Ritual (Nous Sommes Du Soleil)' (Anderson, Howe, Squire, Wakeman, White)

Always the masters of the big finish, 'Ritual' sees the band concluding the album in some style, although – as with the rest of the album – not every moment is successful. What 'Ritual' does have, however, is proper coherence throughout its 22 minutes. The piece begins in fine style, with Squire's thumping bass vying for space with Howe's guitar, and some nice understated synthesiser from Wakeman – the Wilson remix reveals more of this, previously lost in the mix. The bass solo is short, and Howe's reprise of some of his own guitar themes from earlier in the album works nicely. The main theme – 'Nous Somme Du Soleil' (we are of the sun)' is beautiful – one of Anderson's prettiest tunes, with a sort of Gallic 'torch song' feel crossed with some strong harmonies in the Crosby, Stills and Nash style, largely accompanied by Howe's electric sitar, much used on this album. The 'open doors' vocals section does overstay its welcome just a touch but does at least build nicely into the bass/percussion section.

If the track has a problem, it is mainly in the second part of this instrumental section, which features White's percussion, played against his own drum solo, which genuinely feels like it belongs on a live album. Much extended in the band's live performances, there is some visual spectacle here, but on the album, it feels like filler, well played and mixed though it is. Anderson's reprise of the main theme is touching, and the slow build of the track's climax is superb.

Like the 'Revealing Science of God', 'Ritual' has made numerous appearances in the live set, but until the Topographic Tour of 2017/18, the tracks had never appeared together in the same set since the initial *Tales* tour. It was the only piece to make it into the Moraz era, played on the Relayer tour. It was also played on the 2000 *Masterworks Tour* in the USA and on the 2004 World Tour.

Relayer (1974)

Personnel:
Jon Anderson: vocals
Steve Howe: electric and acoustic guitars, pedal steel, vocals
Chris Squire: bass, vocals
Alan White: drums, percussion
Patrick Moraz: keyboards
Produced at New Pipers, Virginia Water on the Rolling Stones Mobile by Yes and Eddie Offord
Tape Operator: Gennaro Rippo.
Co-ordination: Brian Lane.
Released November 1974 (UK). December 1974 (USA)
Highest chart places: UK: 4, USA: 5
Running Time: 40:31

Rick Wakeman left Yes in May 1974 within a few weeks of the final dates on the *Tales* tour, having disliked that album and much of the tour that went with it. He had also had huge success with his second solo album, *Journey To The Centre Of The Earth*. Feeling unable to contribute to the new music the band were developing, he decided to move on.

This gave the band a problem. They couldn't just bring in another Tony Kaye, they needed someone with a technique as well developed as Rick's, not to mention similar technological skills. The band spent several weeks over the course of the early Summer auditioning keyboard players, the highest profile of these being Vangelis, the enigmatic Greek musician. There's an interesting alternative reality where Vangelis is offered and accepts the job. But the musician would have to have toned down his individualistic tendencies to work within such a supposedly democratic band, not to mention the need to become accustomed to travel as a touring musician. Vangelis hated to fly. With the Greek's keyboards still in the studio – a converted garage at New Pipers, Chris Squire's house in Virginia Water in Surrey – Swiss musician Patrick Moraz tried out, and jaws dropped.

Moraz had previously been in a Swiss band called Mainhorse and had then, effectively, replaced Keith Emerson in the Nice, with the band renaming themselves Refugee. A versatile, fluid and flamboyant player, the striking Moraz, with his classical good looks, cleft chin and shock of dark hair, had some of the showmanship of Wakeman but also a strong interest in jazz fusion. This new form of music which blended the harmonic complexity of jazz with the speed and power of rock, developed in parallel with progressive rock in the late 1960s and early 1970s via Miles Davis and later super groups like The Mahavisnu Orchestra and Return To Forever. Despite the styles of neither musician being ideally suited to jazz, Squire and White, in particular, were beginning to draft such influences into the new music being written. Moraz seemed a perfect fit.

Recording began immediately at New Pipers using the Rolling Stones Mobile and continued through the Summer and early Autumn with Eddie Offord again at the helm – for the last time. The band retrenched to the *Close to the Edge* format – with one long side of music and two mid-length pieces, and taken as a whole, *Relayer* is a bold, brash and very rewarding piece of work. However, it is not for the faint-hearted. In 'Gates of Delirium', the band produced the most atonal and difficult work of their career – beloved of many, hated by a minority. 'Sound Chaser' is pure indulgence, a glorious melting pot of mad ideas, while 'To Be Over' has Anderson returning to his theme of 'the river', a truly languid and beautiful piece of music. Overall, the album has a unique tone in the Yes catalogue. It is the only album to have a marked jazz influence outside the odd moment (the scatting on 'Roundabout' being one, of course), but also one which embraces influences – again mainly from Anderson and Howe – in the more atonal classical works of composers like Stravinsky and Shostakovich.

There is a brightness to the sound on the album, which comes not just from the lightness of Moraz's keyboard textures, but also directly from Howe's main choice of guitar, the Fender Broadcaster, an instrument better known for use in Country music, with its fragile, treble-orientated sound. The results are extraordinary.

Once again, the album was understandably given a mixed reception, although it performed well commercially. Played in its entirety during 1974 and 1975, 'To Be Over' was dropped for the Solo tour in 1976 and with Wakeman returning to the band for 1977 dates, the album was understandably dropped entirely except for the 'Soon' section of 'The Gates of Delirium', played in 'The Big Medley' in 1978 and 1979. The other two tracks have never been played since by the whole band, so associated with Patrick Moraz are they, although Steve Howe plays an excellent solo guitar version of 'To Be Over'. 'The Gates of Delirium' has been played on a few tours since – on the Masterworks tour in 2000 and the Symphonic Tour a year later. Frustratingly, from a fan's point of view, a proposed *Relayer* tour in 2020, postponed to 2022 and then cancelled completely, was planned but seems once again to be a long way off. Jon Anderson also played 'Gates' at shows in 2023 with The Band Geeks.

'The Gates of Delirium' (Anderson, Howe, Squire, White, Moraz)
At just under 22 intense minutes, 'The Gates of Delirium' remains the longest individual studio piece in the Yes discography. At a time – in the 21st Century – when long tracks in progressive rock are commonplace, this can often point towards mindless tedium or that the piece is a series of 'bits' strung together (see 'That, That Is', later). Not so this astonishing piece of music. Even more than 'Close to the Edge', this is a track that demands to be the length it is. It would be impossible to class any of this 'song' as 'filler' – it is far too intense a ride for that. 'Gates' was brought to the band by Anderson in rudimentary

form, and played badly on piano – including the 'battle' section. Based very, very loosely on *War And Peace* by Tolstoy, the lyrics are – in my opinion – Anderson's best on any Yes album, beautifully straddling genuine meaning with his usual obliqueness.

The short (two-minute) instrumental introduction is interesting for several reasons. It heralds some themes that we will hear later in the piece; it gives us a glimpse of the form (fearsome) and tone (bright) that Howe will be bringing to the table and finally, it introduces us to Patrick Moraz and this early version of 'soundscaping'. On this track, in particular, his tone and palette are more important than his ability to solo. Having become used to Wakeman's arsenal of instruments, we now get Moraz's. It is very fresh, to the extent that sometimes we don't quite know what instrument is making a particular sound. It's exciting and unsettling too. I genuinely wish he'd made more Yes music.

The first vocal section ('Stand and fight we do consider...') is relatively low key but builds as the acoustic instruments (mandolin or similar) are gradually abandoned and we hear Moraz solo on synthesiser for the first time, and by the five-minute mark, we are in the midst of a more intense, almost hard rocking section. The 'Listen should we fight forever...' section introduces the doubt that everyone feels in war until 'kill or be killed' becomes the more vital emotion. Again, the music builds with Howe playing the main melodic theme and then at eight minutes, 'The fist will run...' unleashes hell ...

At this point, we now have to wait ten minutes before the next vocal passage, yet the track continues twisting and turning, initially with Howe and Moraz taking it in turns to play the melody, with an intense, jazzy rhythm section.

At 10:25, however, the piece shifts into another gear, dominated by Squire's thunderous, fusion bass and we start to hear percussive crashes, as the battle itself gets underway, and Howe's soloing becomes more atonal. The 'war' noises become more powerful, Squire and White keep up a thunderous level of intensity, and then the track threatens to implode, regaining its structure at 12.50 with a superb synthesiser melody line from Moraz – complete with his favourite tool – plenty of pitch bend – until Howe takes up the same theme, switching, via a final bass run from Squire, to pedal steel and it's time for 'Soon'. Many who find the first 16 minutes of 'Gates of Delirium' unpalatable make an exception for this beautiful, uplifting final section. It features some delicious pedal steel from Howe and a wonderfully fragile vocal from Anderson, but Moraz's keyboards should not be underestimated either, initially played on organ, then Mellotron. It is a beautiful piece, and yet it still feels connected to the whole. A single version of 'Soon' was, understandably, released and the band have played this segment of the song live more often than the full piece.

'Sound Chaser' (Anderson, Howe, Squire, White, Moraz)
'From the sublime to the ridiculous' may be a cliché, but here it really is appropriate. 'Sound Chaser' is, in itself, delirious. It is structured like a bad

dream – just as you feel you are settling into the track it takes you somewhere else. It begins with Moraz's Fender Rhodes (and just a touch of Mellotron) and White's percussion – beginning with cymbals, then a drum solo of sorts – dominating. We then hurtle into a lightning-fast, jazzy section, with Howe and Squire playing the same line, then the first vocal section – with Howe, White and Squire playing at full speed, while Moraz and Anderson deal with the actual melody. Squire and Howe keep up the pace before the track breaks down into a hugely indulgent, partially-unaccompanied electric flamenco solo (Al Di Meola territory, this) followed by a slower section, again dominated by Howe and White's timpani. A moment of stillness, a quiet vocal passage from Anderson, then a reprise of the opening, but this time followed by an almost lopsided, swinging section dominated by pedal steel and Mellotron, fast then slow. But wait – then we have Anderson singing 'cha, cha, cha' – a fluid and lengthy Moog solo, underpinned by some astonishing bass from Squire, a final fast section which seems to feature every theme in the song at the same time, one more set of 'cha, cha's' and we're out ....

What should we make of 'Sound Chaser'? I love it, but I also recognise that it – rather than (say) 'The Ancient' – probably represents progressive rock at its most indulgent. While it is Howe and Moraz that get to play the 'flashy' bits, the real stars are White and Squire. White is allowed to hit many, many different pieces of percussion, loud and quiet, while Squire – who played with a pick, let us not forget – produces some runs so fast that one almost wonders if they were speeded up in the studio. But we know they weren't. Only in the years 1974 or 1975 could a track like this have been created – and released – and still get into the top ten of the album charts on both sides of the Atlantic. Oh, and it opened the set for almost two years of touring, as well. It is mind-altering, bonkers stuff.

'To Be Over' (Anderson, Howe, Squire, White, Moraz)
Back to the sublime again with this glorious, unsung classic. I say unsung because it can sometimes be overlooked after the bluster and flash of the two previous tracks. However, this is a place of serenity, a piece of music that really 'flows downstream', led initially by Howe's electric sitar and Moraz's synthesiser, but dominated by Howe's pedal steel and Fender Broadcaster combo, as the rest of the album has been. Yes always know how to end an album, and the gentle build towards the final vocal section and Moraz's lovely Moog solo feel like a prelude to the climax of 'Awaken' three years later, but here the piece fades to nothing. It is a poised and supremely controlled masterpiece.

The Solo Albums

While the albums themselves – in terms of a track-by-track analysis at least –
are beyond the scope of this book, it is worth looking at them in brief, since
they represent two years in the history of that band.

The period from autumn 1974 to Late Summer 1976 represents a period of
sporadic touring, mainly in the USA. As often happens with a band of this
apparent stature, riding a wave of excellent album sales, they made a joint
decision – indulged by label Atlantic – to make solo albums, recorded around
the touring, rather than rush into the studio (or maybe Squire's garage) and
make another album with Moraz.

...So, the five musicians, with occasional help from their bandmates, went
their own separate ways to put their individual ideas onto vinyl. The whole
process could have been a trainwreck, but actually, all five of the resultant
albums have plenty of merit. Indeed, the process produced one classic album
'for the ages', two almost as good, an underrated gem and a misfire with
plenty still to admire. But which is which?

Steve Howe – Beginnings

Released November 1975
Chart placings. UK: 22, US: 63

First out of the gate at the end of 1975 was Howe's *Beginnings* album.
The record has had a real kicking from Yes fans over the years due to
the quality of Howe's vocals, and the overall poor standard of the song
material. You will find no revisionism here (not yet, at least), sadly. The
problem seems to be that the keys are at the top end of Howe's range as
a lead vocalist, and the melodies that he is asking himself to sing would
challenge any vocalist, let alone someone with as little experience as the
guitarist. Only on the final song, 'Break Away From It All' does his singing
work, since they are sung as choral vocals in what is a mainly instrumental
piece. There are several instrumental pleasures, however. The title track –
orchestrated by Patrick Moraz – is a wonder, as is the jaunty 'The Nature of
the Sea'. Alan White and Bill Bruford also guest. Much better was to follow
for Howe, thankfully, with an excellent 1979 follow-up in *The Steve Howe
Album* , which led to a long – and at time of writing unbroken – string of
high-quality solo efforts.

Chris Squire – Fish Out of Water

Released December 1975
Chart placings. UK: 25, US: 69

Next out was Chis Squire's remarkable *Fish Out of Water*, a flawed
masterpiece if ever there was one. Yes fans always knew Squire could sing,
and here he shows how adept he could be as a lead vocalist. There's a LOT
of bass on the album, as one might expect, but here it mainly serves that
material, which is very good. Terrific support comes from Moraz (again)

and Bill Bruford, who drums throughout and is terrific, and Andrew Pryce Jackman, whose orchestrations are exquisite.

If the album has a flaw, it's because, with only five songs in total, the two longer pieces arguably overstay their welcome. 'Silently Falling' is thrilling up to the seven-minute mark, and might have been better ending there, while album closer 'Lucky Seven', which ends as an orchestral canon, feels like it is ending around eight and a half minutes, yet builds again to another big finish. It's bold, certainly, but it doesn't quite work to these ears.

These flaws aside, it's terrific.

Alan White – Ramshackled
Released March 1976
Chart placings. UK: 41, USA: DNC
White's album was the next to arrive. The recipient of quite a bit of disdain from Yes fans for the cardinal sin of not being very progressive, if any of the five solo albums is worthy of reappraisal (sorry, Steve), it's this one. True, its songs have a mid-70s pop-soul vibe that has not worn especially well. But, on an album where most attention has gone on the sweet but inconsequential 'Spring-Song of Innocence' simply due to the presence of Anderson and Howe, several tracks have gone relatively unloved. Try the poppy 'One Way Rag' or the fun big band jazz of 'Avakak', and the expansive pop-jazz of closer 'Darkness'. White plays drums only, so most of the creativity lies in the hands of keyboard player Kenny Craddock and guitarist Pete Kirtley, who, it has to be said, do an excellent job. In short, don't believe the naysayers. Give the album a go yourself. You might be pleasantly surprised.

Patrick Moraz – The Story of i
Released April 1976
Chart placings. UK: 28, USA: 132
Sometimes called just *Patrick Moraz,* this features no Yes members – past or present – but brings together some top-of-the-range jazz fusion players like Jeff Berlin and Alphonse Mouzon, with the singing and songwriting talents of John McBurnie, who had previously been in Jackson Heights – a post-Nice project of Moraz's compatriot in Refugee, Lee Jackson (still with it?).

The result is a bonkers but hugely endearing two sides that mixes Brazilian rhythms with pop, prog and fusion. The production is a little flat, but even with that, it's terrific – if not for the faint-hearted. Moraz has gone on to a lengthy solo career, but only this and its post-Yes follow-up *Out in the Sun* have charted.

Jon Anderson – Olias of Sunhillow
Released July 1976
Chart placings: UK: 8, USA: 47
... and finally, we come to the most successful of the five albums and the longest in arriving. This completely unique album is one of a kind, created

entirely within the imagination of the vocalist, and with every instrument
played by him. As we know, Anderson's instrumental skills are fairly
rudimentary, so his ability to record an album without other musicians
severely restricts what he could play. But he really made it work for him.
Based around a mystical fantasy storyline, Anderson's object was to create an
other-worldly musical world. It challenged his mental health as he layered
guitars, keyboards, percussion and vocals to create his vision. The results are
astonishing – thoroughly progressive, yet not 'rock' as such. There are no kit
drums, and the bass playing is rhythmic and rudimentary. The character of
the piece comes from Anderson's tuneful writing, his chanted vocals and the
wealth of keyboard and percussive textures. The album performed well in the
UK, reaching the top ten.

Having toured for a year and a half on the back of the *Relayer* album, Yes
tried to 'tour' the solo albums for the summer of 1976, with songs from each
of the band member's albums except Anderson's. However, over the next
week or so, the solo songs were gradually dropped and eventually, 'Ritual'
came back into the set, and the experiment was abandoned.

Above: A windswept and chilly-looking band, pictured in early 1974 just prior to Wakeman's first departure. (*Alamy*)

Below: The current lineup pictured at the Palladium in 2018. Howe, Davison, Downes, Sherwood, Schellen. (*Stephen Lambe*)

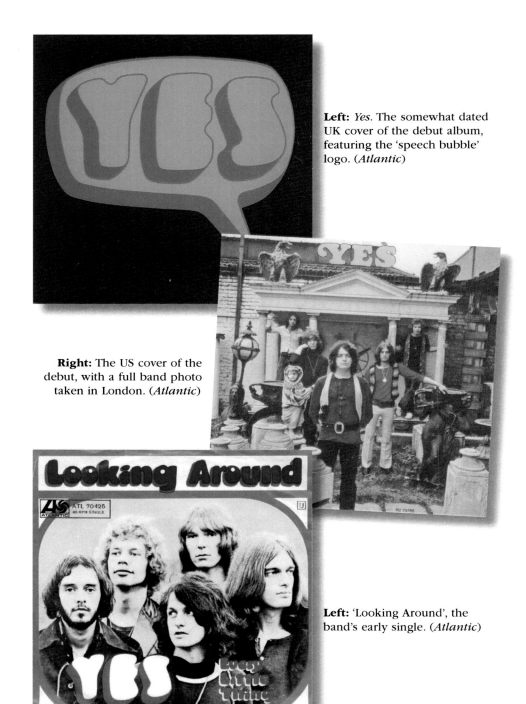

Left: *Yes*. The somewhat dated UK cover of the debut album, featuring the 'speech bubble' logo. (*Atlantic*)

Right: The US cover of the debut, with a full band photo taken in London. (*Atlantic*)

Left: 'Looking Around', the band's early single. (*Atlantic*)

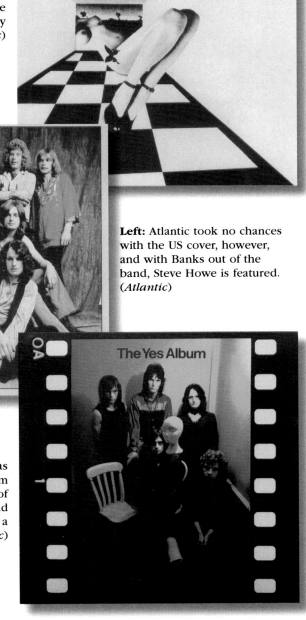

TIME AND A WORD/YES

Right: *Time and a Word*. The bold UK cover was designed by Laurence Sackman. (*Atlantic*)

Left: Atlantic took no chances with the US cover, however, and with Banks out of the band, Steve Howe is featured. (*Atlantic*)

Right: *The Yes Album*. This was the band's breakthrough album in the UK. Note the plaster of Kaye's ankle, the result of a road accident on the way back from a gig in Basingstoke. (*Atlantic*)

Left: A lanky squire during an early German TV appearance.

Right: A bearded Peter Banks playing his trusty Rickenbacker.

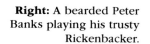

Left: Tony Kaye on Hammond during a performance of 'Survival' on German TV.

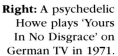

Right: A psychedelic Howe plays 'Yours In No Disgrace' on German TV in 1971.

Left: Jon Anderson, already a performing veteran in his mid-20s.

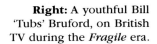

Right: A youthful Bill 'Tubs' Bruford, on British TV during the *Fragile* era.

Left: Roger Dean's Yes debut the remarkable cover for *Fragile*. The album marked the debut of Rick Wakeman. The spacecraft became Dean's 'signature'. (*Atlantic*)

Right: Dean followed that album with the bold cover for *Close To The Edge*. The classic Yes logo made its appearance for the first time. (*Atlantic*)

Left: The cover of *Tales From Topographic Oceans*, is, if anything, even more distinctive. It's a remarkable window into the tone of this flawed album. (*Atlantic*)

Right: The fourth Dean cover was for *Relayer,* Patrick Moraz's only album with the band. (*Atlantic*)

Left: A moment of relaxation for the Moraz-era band. (*Getty Images*)

Right: All change for *Going For The One*, with Hipgnosis handling the cover design and Wakeman back in the band. (*Atlantic*)

Left: The harmony was short-lived. *Tormato* found the band struggling with arrangements and the group's overall direction. (*Atlantic*)

Right: *Drama*. After some aborted sessions in Paris, the band fragmented, with Anderson and Wakeman replaced by Trevor Horn and Geoff Downes. It was to be quite a year! (*Atlantic*)

Below: A colourful publicity shot of the *Drama*-era band. *(Atlantic)*

Right: Yes dissolved from 1980 to 1983, but made a triumphant return with the ultra-modern *90125* at the end of 1983, with Anderson coaxed back into the band. (*Atco*)

Left: The man that made the *90125* lineup sexy, Trevor Rabin.

Right: The colour scheme for the CD release of *Big Generator*, the band's laborious 1987 follow-up to *90125*. (*Atco*)

Left: *Anderson, Bruford, Wakeman, Howe.* Though not technically a Yes album, it certainly has the Yes 'spirit', even if some of the music betrays its origins as a Jon Anderson project. (*Arista*)

Right: *Union.* The album that brought ABWH and 'Yes West' together in an album that pleased almost nobody, but still has a few decent moments. (*Arista*)

Left: *Talk.* In another radical design shift, the album featured a new logo by artist Peter Max. It didn't 'take' and nor did the lineup that recorded the album. (*Eagle*)

Right: *Keys To Ascension,* with a slightly bland Dean cover. The two studio tracks are decent, but better was to come. (*Castle Communications*)

Left: *Keys To Ascension 2*. More studio recordings produced the fabulous 'Mind Drive' and a better-integrated Rick Wakeman. (*Castle Communications*)

Right: *Open Your Eyes*. A dull cover, with suggestions of the 1969 debut. The contents are much derided, but the album is much better than its reputation suggests. (*Eagle*)

Left: *The Ladder*. A harmonious band produces an equally harmonious, but mediocre album. (*Eagle*)

Right: *Magnification*. A disappointing cover, considering the quality of the computer-generated artwork by Bob Gesca inside the CD booklet. (*Eagle*)

Left: *Fly From Here*. A bold, bright cover from Roger Dean illustrates the album that saw Oliver Wakeman replaced by Geoff Downes. (*Frontiers*)

Right: *Heaven And Earth*. Given that this was Chris Squire's last album with the band and Jon Davison's first, the results are almost tragically substandard. (*Frontiers*)

Left: *Fly From Here The Return Trip*. Benoit David was replaced by Trevor Horn, to a mixed reaction, but the remix and tightened arrangements were something of an improvement on the 2011 original. (*Pledge Music*)

Below: The post-Anderson lineup circa 2009-10, featuring Oliver Wakeman and Benoit David.

Left: *From A Page*. A surprise mini album but given official status. The music was compiled by Oliver Wakeman from unreleased recordings from the early *Fly From Here* sessions. (*Yes 97 LLC*)

Right: *The Quest*. Released in 2021, these were Alan White's last recordings with the band. (*InsideOut*)

Left: *Mirror To The Sky*. Released in 2023, this was in some ways an advance on *The Quest*, although the material was arguably weaker. (*InsideOut*)

Right: One in a series of lush, attractive concert programmes. This one is from the *Going For The One* tour in 1977. (*Bruce Strickland*)

Above: The *Tormato* tour programme from 1978, your author's first even Yes experience. (*Stephen Lambe*)

Right: Seeing Yes at The DeMontford Hall in Leicester in 1975 would have set you back a whopping £1.25. By the 1978 Wembley shows, ticket prices had gone up to £5. (*Bruce Strickland*)

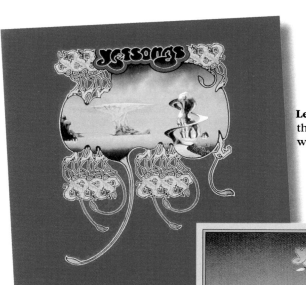

Left: *Yessongs*. The front cover to the band's 1973 live triple album was not Dean's finest. (*Atlantic*)

Right: *Yesshows*. Meanwhile, this double album documented the 1975 to 1978 period, with mixed results musically but a nicer cover painting. (*Atlantic*)

Left: *Yesterdays*. Dean's cover for the band's 1974 compilation paid lip service to the UK *Time And A Word* cover. (*Atlantic*)

Going for the One (1977)

Personnel:
Jon Anderson: vocals, harp Chris Squire: bass, vocals
Steve Howe: electric and acoustic guitar, pedal steel, vocals
Alan White: drums, tuned percussion
Rick Wakeman: keyboards, piano, polymoog, church organ
The Richard Williams Singers: choir
Produced at Mountain Studios, Montreux, Switzerland by Yes. Engineer John
Timperley, assisted by David Richards
Executive Producer: Brian Lane
Released: July 1977.
Highest chart places: UK: 1, USA: 8
Running time: 38:49

By the time the band – including Patrick Moraz – returned to the studio to
record their next album, it had been two years since Relayer. All five members
had released solo albums and there had been two long – and lucrative –
Summer tours, mainly playing stadiums and arenas in the USA. Choosing to
record in Switzerland – Moraz's home country – for tax reasons must have
been thrilling for him, yet within a few weeks, he was out of the band.

Supposedly, he wasn't gelling musically, yet there is also a suggestion of
manoeuvring by Brian Lane, manager both of the band and Rick Wakeman.
Lane's executive producer credit is no coincidence, and nor, one suspects was
Wakeman's reinstatement following the recent dip in his solo career.

With Rick back as a 'session player', initially, at least, the first question often
asked is 'how much Moraz is on the album?' This is impossible to answer,
he certainly has no writing credits, yet Moraz lays claim to a big part of the
initial development of the arrangements for the songs, which is likely. With
Wakeman back and enthusiastic about the more concise, melodic approach
evident in the music, there were other changes too. Eddie Offord was
out, replaced by engineer John Timperley, best known for his 1960s work
with Cream and the Beatles. Gone also was Roger Dean, with the album
given a striking, modern cover by Hipgnosis. Frankly, although the cover,
with a naked man looking up at angular, skyscraper-style objects against a
blue sky (or blue background, at least) is hard to forget, it has dated very
badly compared to the timeless surrealism of Dean's early 70s covers – still
considered iconic today.

Containing three pieces broadly considered 'songs', a longer, more esoteric
piece in 'Turn of the Century' and the 15-minute 'Awaken', the album itself has
a reputation as a masterpiece: the last 'great' Yes album. It is hard to disagree,
yet it does have its frustrations. Offord is badly missed, and the final mix seems
very thin – even on the re-mastered Rhino version, and it is drenched in reverb.
That it is considered a great album despite this fundamental flaw demonstrates
the quality of the material, the arrangements and the playing. Like the best

albums by Yes – and indeed by anyone – what makes *Going for the One* really special is the unique atmosphere it creates. There is no other album like it, and it's hard to compare its individual five tracks with anything else in the catalogue. Its reputation has also been enhanced because it is so well thought of by the band itself, deemed by all concerned a happy experience, with Wakeman's eventual return as a full-time member the icing on the cake.

Largely well-received by the press on its release, the album performed well – reaching number one in the UK album charts – without reaching the massive worldwide status of *Fragile* or *Close to the Edge*, and was assisted in the UK at least by the rather unexpected success of 'Wonderous Stories' – a top ten hit single in 1977.

'Going for the One' (Anderson)

The band go for the jugular from the first moment with some searing pedal steel guitar from Steve Howe, an unusual usage of this instrument more regularly associated with country music. The riffing at the start of the second verse is particularly impressive. Wakeman has fun with a funky piano part, but otherwise, it's Anderson's song, an extended 'horse racing' metaphor leading into a fairly obvious dig at his 'hippy-dippy' public image and the difficulty with coming up with lyrics. Despite the aggression of the track, there's still time for plenty of Yes-ish subtlety, with a 'Siberian Khatru' word list, some dancing bass – and some inventive backing vocals – from Squire, and the sort of drumming from White that would never have been contemplated in the Bruford era. A good piece played live, as you might expect, it has dropped in and out of the band's set over the last 40 years, possibly due to its relative brevity.

'Turn of the Century' (Anderson, Howe, White)

Struggling with the emotional angst of being sixteen, this was probably my favourite song by the band for a long time. Lyrically, and tonally, this delightful piece of music is shamelessly romantic, even for Anderson, never one to hold back on his feelings. It tells the age-old story of a man who loses his love, and is compelled to reproduce her in sculpture, only to find his passion animating the statue. It is one of those pieces where the instrumentation enhances the story perfectly, building tension and release at exactly the right moments.

Howe's classical guitar at the start is beautiful and Anderson's reverb-heavy vocal pulls at the heart strings with Wakeman's keyboards subtle and distant, joined my some delicate percussion from White and Squire's backing vocals. Halfway through, Wakeman's piano takes over, joined by Howe's guitar and Squire's bass, with White switching to timpani. At one point, at around 5.05, the arrangement almost trips up on itself, but then the instruments come together in unison, building to the final, hugely uplifting vocal section before ending on Howe's classical guitar once again.

A difficult piece to pull off live, the song has never been a regular part of the live set, but has made a few appearances, on the 2004 world tour and also as part of the 1996 *Keys To Ascension* concerts.

'Parallels' (Squire)
Only Yes would attempt this – an entire track, with the band rocking out, and Wakeman playing only one instrument: a huge church organ recorded at St.Martin's Church, Vevey in Switzerland. That the band could achieve this – he played via a high-speed phone line – is thanks to the technological sophistication of the Swiss. This was 1976, let us not forget. As a song, this rocker from Chris Squire is powerful stuff, including some wonderful lead guitar from Howe. Wakeman's church organ is certainly worth the effort, giving the track a tone that would be hard to achieve on the Hammond, and the organ 'break' in the middle of the song is very effective. Howe can't have traded lead lines with such an instrument very often. The three-part vocal towards the end of the song – with Squire on the left of the stereo, Anderson in the middle and Howe on the right – is also very effective.

Given that it's a big, rocking track, 'Parallels' has not been played live particularly often, probably due to the inability to produce the church organ sound on a Hammond. When the band played it on the *Going for the One* tour – when it opened the show – Wakeman played his mid-song solo on Minimoog, to really good effect, as can be heard on the *Yesshows* live album.

'Wonderous Stories' (Anderson)
A top ten hit single in the UK, this delicate and tuneful piece is a delightfully evocative song from Anderson. Howe plays Vachalia, last heard on 'Your Move', and Wakeman solos effectively on Polymoog. Like 'Turn of the Century', this song shows how well Yes could do 'delicate' even playing as a full band, although there are no drums on this studio version. It is a perfectly constructed three minutes 50 seconds. Something of a throw-away track in a live setting, it has popped in and out of the live set on a regular basis, with the band feeling no obligation to play it on every tour, despite its status in the UK, unlike 'Owner Of A Lonely Heart' .

'Awaken' (Anderson, Howe)
While *Going for the One* rarely wins 'Yes greatest album' polls, the track that tends to come first every time is this fifteen-and-a-half minute masterpiece, which shows off everything that makes Yes, and indeed progressive rock, so compelling when it is done well. It has its neo-classical moments – particularly Wakeman's piano introduction and also the slow build of the church organ in the instrumental mid-section. But it's a masterpiece of construction, from the ensemble virtuosity of the opening full-band section, with Howe and Wakeman in complete harmony (unlike *Tormato*). Howe, once again, is in astonishing form, as he is throughout the album, and here

the church organ is integrated amongst the other instruments before coming into its own during the slow build of percussion, organ and Anderson's harp. The choir is also a masterstroke, sung by The Richard Williams Singers with an arrangement by Rick Wakeman. There is huge tension in this mid-section, as the rest of the band enter gradually against Wakeman's church organ, first Squire's bass, then Howe's delicate electric guitar building as White switches back to drums and Anderson sings the 'Master of Images' section. The piece continues to build in intensity towards the final, ecstatic 'Like The Time I Ran Away' section and Howe's final electric guitar coda.

'Awaken' is an incredibly effective live piece, and a powerful set closer. On *The Ladder* tour, the band sometimes showered the audience with ticker-tape as shown on the live DVD, but again there are many live recordings to choose from, and like 'And You And I', it is a real show-stopper. Although some compromises were needed to re-arrange the track to be played live, few liberties have been taken with the arrangement overall until, that is, Yes, featuring Anderson, Rabin, Wakeman put in some effective percussion-based embellishments into their otherwise-faithful rendition in 2017 and 2018.

Related tracks
'Montreux's Theme' (Howe, Squire, Anderson, White)
A rather aimless but pleasant, almost jazzy instrumental dominated by Howe with Anderson (by the sound of it) on rhythm guitar and barely any keyboards except possibly some organ in the background.

'Vevey' (Anderson, Wakeman)
Anderson on (slightly hamfisted) harp and Wakeman on church organ improvise a few tunes. The organ is lovely. The harp is less so. The section on the Rhino re-master is rather better than the two snippets on the *Yesyears* boxed set. Definitely 'listen once' music.

'Amazing Grace' (trad, arranged Squire)
A part of Squire's bass solo on some tours, this is a straight version of the main melody of the traditional hymn, played on an over-driven bass guitar and bass pedals. As a track in its own right, it's a bit pointless.

Tormato (1978)

Personnel:

Jon Anderson: vocals, Alvarez 10-string guitar

Chris Squire: Rickenbacker bass, bass pedals, piano, Gibson Thunderbird bass, vocals

Steve Howe: Les Paul Custom, Martin 00045, Gibson 'the Les Paul', Spanish Guitar, Fender Broadcaster, Mandolin, Gibson 175D, vocals

Alan White: drums, percussion, drum synthesiser

Rick Wakeman: Birotron, Hammond Organ, Polymoog, Harpsichord, piano, RMI computer keyboard

Damion Anderson: vocal on 'Circus of Heaven'

Arranged and produced by Yes

Engineers Geoff Young and Nigel Luby

Orchestral arrangement on 'Onward' and string arrangement on 'Madrigal' by Andrew Pryce Jackman

Recorded at Advision. Additional recording and mixing at RAK studios.

Executive Producer: Brian Lane

Released: September 1978.

Highest chart places: UK: 8, USA: 10

Running time: 41:35

Given its status in most polls as one of the poorer Yes albums, *Tormato* holds some sort of mythical status amongst a set minority of Yes fans. It was well-favoured enough to warrant its own book by *Yes Music Podcast* head honcho Kevin Mulryne, whose 2023 tome *Yes : The Tormato Story* was published in 2023. Oliver Wakeman (who will feature later in our story) cites it as his favourite Yes album, and while there is no doubt it's 'problematic', there is much to its story that makes its creation and release far more interesting to Yes aficionados than more harmonious releases, such as the one that proceeded it.

As for your author, *Tormato* was my 'entry' album to Yes. I saw the band live for the first time at Wembley Arena one month after the album was released, and it still holds a special place in my heart. And yet I have often wondered how the harmonious band that recorded and toured *Going for the One* began to sour so quickly.

Despite some personal sentimental value, the album remains hugely flawed. Why?

Many commentators have rightly pointed out a problem with some of the arrangements on *Tormato*, in that Steve Howe and Rick Wakeman seem to be clashing and fighting for the same space in the mix. For the first time on a Yes album, both musicians had equal status in the band. On *Fragile* and *Close to the Edge*, Wakeman was a junior member in a developing band, while on *Topographic Oceans*, when he might have played a fuller part (when, ironically, he was given a one-fifth writing credit on the whole album), he was not fully engaged in the material presented by Howe and Anderson.

On *Going for the One,* he was a hired hand, adding fairy dust to already-established material. But here he was, a big star and part of a band as an equal member. He was entitled to his share of the limelight. This means that with no long pieces in the style of 'Awaken', some tracks were over-filled with Howe and Wakeman soloing against each other.

The album is also held up as an example of how not to self-produce, suggesting that the 'many hands on the fader' approach produced a lot of compromises and an overly compressed sound mix. Certainly, the mix has a compressed, cluttered feel, more in need of a remix than the earlier, classic albums so expertly and sensitively handled by Steven Wilson, although it is believed that the original multi-track recordings may be unavailable. This is not helped by some rather dated keyboard sounds, from the 'alien' effects in 'Arriving UFO' to Alan White's syn-drum in 'Release, Release'. Although the idea that punk and new wave thrust progressive rock aside is a myth, it is also clear that Atlantic were keen to receive a rockier album with briefer songs to take advantage of the changing market. To a certain extent, they got it.

Rick Wakeman was also favouring two keyboard instruments that were to become obsolete fairly quickly. The first was the Polymoog, an early polyphonic synthesiser manufactured until 1980. Wakeman was an early adopter of this instrument, understandably so as he has a close association with the Moog organisation, yet in this case, he backed the wrong horse, with Sequential Circuit's Prophets 5 and 10 becoming the more ubiquitous analogue instruments in the late 70s and early 80s, before digital synthesisers took hold of the market. The other instrument used extensively on *Tormato* was the Birotron, an advanced version of the Mellotron. Again, Wakeman was directly involved in the development of this instrument, which, while it was certainly innovative and a huge advance on the Mellotron, suffered from rapidly increased costs so that, in the end, only a few were ever manufactured.

And yet there is still much to admire in *Tormato*. At its heart, the album is saved by some excellent songwriting – in this aspect, it is probably an advance on *Going for the One* – and some very fine playing from the band. So, while it will never be considered a classic by all but a small proportion of Yes fans, it is far from the disaster it is often cracked up to be.

'Future Times' (Anderson, Howe, Squire, Wakeman, White) **/ 'Rejoice'** (Anderson)
Often held up as one of the tracks on which Howe and Wakeman clash, 'Future Times' is certainly a busy piece, with Squire's harmonized bass also fighting for attention. In the opening instrumental section, before the vocals arrive, Howe's Les Paul and Wakeman's Polymoog weave around each other. In another universe, one of these lines – probably Wakeman's synth – might have been ditched without causing any damage to the track at all. However, I think the arrangement actually works pretty well, with both instruments

often in unison. If anything, at just over four minutes, it is too short. Squire's bass in 'Rejoice' hints – and it is only a hint – at reggae, but the rest of the track is a showcase for Wakeman's synthesiser work. Both these short pieces are full of excellent ideas, dispensed with much too quickly. The band played these songs early in the set on the 1978-1979 *Tormato* world tour, and Jon Anderson took the reggae influence in 'Rejoice' and accentuated it when he played the song in his Yes medley on the *Song of Seven* solo tour.

'Don't Kill the Whale' (Anderson, Squire)

Mainly penned by Squire, and presented to the band as a finished piece, this is a fairly straightforward song with a worthy, ecological subject. Howe's Les Paul is again prominent, and the Birotron can be heard on the verses in all its compressed glory. The band have played this live occasionally, particularly in the 2010s. It was a minor hit in the UK, reaching number 36 ahead of the album release in September 1978. Anderson also played a rearrangement of the song (combined with Led Zeppelin's 'Kashmir' of all pieces) on tour in 2022 and 2023.

'Madrigal' (Anderson, Wakeman)

Rick Wakeman's excursions on harpsichord are rare but always excellent. Utterly charming, this simple piece features Wakeman on the instrument and Steve Howe on Spanish guitar. Add to that a typically 'out there' lyric from Anderson and some beautiful harmony vocals, and that's all you need, really. One of Yes' most delightful short pieces, it was played live during 1978, and also by the 2020s line up as a 'deep cut'. For more details on the harpsichord, see Kevin Mulryne's book.

'Release, Release' (Anderson, White, Squire)

Yes have never been afraid to 'rock out', even prior to the Rabin era. However, for the five and a half minutes of 'Release, Release', they showed that even they could play with blues chords once in a while. The song is an up-tempo rocker, driven by some terrific drumming from Alan White, and dominated by Steve Howe's Fender Broadcaster, his weapon of choice on *Relayer*. However, it is a Yes trademark – inventive and beautifully-crafted vocal arrangements – that are most impressive here. Only Wakeman's Polymoog soloing, pretty much throughout the early verses, seems out of place. The drum solo / fake crowd noise section is an interesting (if controversial) touch, though leading into a guitar solo, it does build some tension before the 'straight jacket, freedom's march' vocal section. Wakeman is better used during his solo late in the song. Powerful and exuberant, this is, in the main, terrific stuff, perhaps a precursor of the rockier approach to be found two years later on *Drama*. Ironically, for a song that begs to be played live, it was dropped quite early on in 1978 as the vocals were too high for Anderson to sing without putting unnecessary pressure on his voice.

'Arriving UFO' (Anderson, Howe, Wakeman)
Another track played live occasionally on the *Tormato* the tour, but completely ignored since, is this rather quirky and dated piece. Riffing on the then-current craze for all things extra-terrestrial, heralded by Steve Spielberg's *Close Encounters of the Third Kind*, the tone of this piece also suggests 'Teakbois' from Anderson, Bruford, Wakeman, Howe eleven years later, a track that is equally derided. Both Wakeman's Polymoog chords and Alan White's syn drums have dated quite badly. Amongst the silliness – and I remember we thought it a bit silly even at the time – is some terrific bass from Chris Squire and a great Les Paul solo from Howe that deserves to be on a better piece of music. Again, if you must delve a little more deeply into this interesting but rather silly piece, Kevin Mulryne's book will tell you all you need to know.

'Circus of Heaven' (Anderson)
Speaking of silly, the quirkiness continues with this cloying piece of kitsch Bossa Nova, with hints of The Beatles, from the pen of Jon Anderson. Such high-concept music is difficult to pull off, and some inventive playing from the band cannot save it. Jon's son Damion provides the spoken word section at the end. The song was played live in 1978 and 1979.

'Onward' (Squire)
Another big shift in tone heralds this beautiful, romantic tune from Squire. Although a million miles from the early 70s Yes sound, it remains a minor classic. It took on swathes of added meaning following Squire's death in 2015, as the band played it on tape at the start of shows – a single spotlight shining on his Rickenbacker – as a tribute to their departed colleague. The song is a triumph of simplicity, with an orchestral arrangement from Andrew Pryce Jackman and an unusual guitar line from Howe, which complements Squire's rising and falling bass line perfectly. Anderson – as usual – sings like he means every moment and Squire himself also provides one of his most charming harmony vocals – a perfect illustration of why his voice blended so well with Anderson's.

'On the Silent Wings of Freedom' (Anderson, Squire)
Squire is also heavily featured on the album's final eight-minute track, possibly the album's strongest 'full band' piece, soloing over some great drumming from White, while both Howe and Wakeman embellish inventively. While the song itself would not survive the 1978-1979 tour, until revived in a somewhat truncated and unsatisfactory form in 2022, Squire's bass riff would appear in the 'White-Fish' duo section of shows for many years to come. The slow atmospheric section before the final build towards the album's powerful climax is the best calling card for the Birotron on the album and leads into Wakeman's best moment – an extended and thrilling Polymoog solo. A strong end to a somewhat disjointed album.

Related tracks
'Abilene' (Howe)
A rather turgid, throwaway pop song written by Steve Howe, which feels like a demo fleshed out quickly when an extra song was needed. Howe solos nicely, but the rest of the band appear disinterested. The song was the B-side of the 'Don't Kill the Whale' single.

'Money' (Squire, Anderson, White, Wakeman)
More throwaway stuff, this time a piece of good-time boogie during which Rick Wakeman performs an almost unintelligible impersonation of Denis Healey, then Chancellor of the Exchequer in the Labour government, which lasts, somewhat tortuously, for the entire song.

The Paris Sessions and related tracks (1979)

Personnel:
Jon Anderson: vocals, guitar
Chris Squire: bass, vocals
Steve Howe: guitars, vocals
Alan White: drums, percussion
Rick Wakeman: keyboards
Produced by Roy Thomas Baker
Recorded Autumn 1979, Paris.

Following the in the round tour of 1978-79, the band took a short break and then convened in Paris with the famed – some might even say notorious – Roy Thomas Baker producing them. The sessions did not go well, with the band factionalised into Howe, Squire and White against Anderson and Wakeman.

Recording broke up before Christmas when White broke his foot roller skating. As the resulting tracks remained unreleased for many years except via bootleg versions, they have had far more attention than they frankly deserve. We will add to the column inches here, by discussing – briefly – the versions that were finally released.

What is clear is that the tracks we have are very Anderson / Wakeman heavy with some lacklustre bass and drums and so little Howe that he may as well not be in the band. Indeed, Howe is almost entirely absent, but that may be down to his customary habit of recording his guitar parts separately. Or he hated the material. Or both. It is hard to know whether any of these songs might have been salvageable, but you can almost feel the boredom and animosity, giving the pieces a sort of macabre fascination. The writing credits shown are the 'official' ones, although it's more likely that most were written by Anderson and Wakeman only.

'Dancing Through The Light' (Anderson, Howe, Squire, Wakeman, White)
Source: Rhino re-master of *Drama*
Yes go disco! I guess they had to at some point. This rudimentary piece was the inspiration for the Drama track 'Dance Through the Light', and you can certainly hear it in this version, which contains no guitar and a vocoder-style vocal. Squire's bass is actually rather well done, even if White sounds a bit less comfortable with the disco style – he's solid in a rock sort of way. Not awful, but not much more than a demo.

'Golden Age' (Anderson, Howe, Squire, Wakeman, White)
Source: Rhino re-master of *Drama*
Again, a piece with some promise, but this sounds like a demo produced by Anderson and Wakeman, and the song itself doesn't really hang together. The

drums and bass don't sound convincing, and the guitar certainly sounds like Anderson rather than Howe. Wakeman used some of his parts for his *Rock 'n' Roll Prophet* album, while Anderson used other parts for 'Some Are Born' on his *Song of Seven* solo album.

'Tango' (Anderson, Howe, Squire, Wakeman, White)
Source: *In A Word* boxed set
The tango-inspired verse is a terrible idea, but when the track leaps into life it's not bad at all. Anderson's vocal is clearly a guide one only. This is another piece that might have been developed into something decent and again, this is Wakeman-heavy and has no guitar.

'In The Tower' (Anderson, Howe, Squire, Wakeman, White)
Source: Rhino re-master of *Drama*
An almost ecclesiastical organ backs a rather aimless Anderson melody, with some lacklustre drums and no bass or guitar to speak of. It's a demo and little more than that.

'Friend Of A Friend' (Anderson, Howe, Squire, Wakeman, White)
Source: Rhino re-master of *Drama*
Again, this is somewhat aimless stuff that might have developed into something more interesting. At least the whole band seems to be playing on this one, even if it's pretty rough and there's only rhythm guitar on it. There's a nice Wakeman keyboard run towards the end, but I'm clutching at straws, really.

'Never Done Before' (Anderson, Howe, Squire, Wakeman, White)
Source: *In A Word* boxed set
If in trouble, try to sound like The Beatles. Again, this has a nice honky-tonk piano solo from Wakeman and nothing else of note. Howe is again present, but only just.

A version of 'Everybody Loves You', which wound up on *Song Of Seven* in splendid shape, is also available on some bootlegs but has never been released officially.

Tormato Outtakes (probably)
The Rhino *Tormato* remaster contains a number of pieces of varying professionalism and quality that are most probably the additional songs recorded at RAK Studios after the main sessions at Advision had been completed for that album. Other versions of tracks like 'Money' have been made available on bootlegs, though these versions offer up very little extra information, and only the officially released versions are dealt with here. Some of these songs are clearly demos and may just have easily been recorded at the home of the composer.

'Picasso' (Anderson)
Source: Rhino re-master of *Tormato*
This is slight but rather lovely, and the whole band sound like they mean it, so this probably comes from the *Tormato* sessions.

'Some Are Born' (Anderson)
Source: Rhino re-master of *Tormato*
An early but very recognisable version of the song that finally appeared on *Song Of Seven*. It is not a concise as the final version, but the bare bones are there.

'You Can Be Saved' (Squire)
Source: Rhino re-master of *Tormato*
A nice song from Squire here presented again in rudimentary form, sung as an untidy duet between Anderson and Squire.

'High' (Howe)
Source: Rhino re-master of *Tormato*
A rough-as-old-boots song from Howe – basically a riff with some sketchy vocals and drums. The guitar sounds for all the world like it's trying to play 'Heartsong' by Gordon Giltrap, but hearing Jon Anderson sing in the bath might be better than this.

'Days – demo' (Anderson)
Source: Rhino re-master of *Tormato*
An *a capella* version of the piece that ended up on Song Of Seven. It actually works nicely sung like this.

'Countryside' (Anderson, Howe, Squire, White)
Source: Rhino re-master of *Tormato*
Not bad, actually, thanks to the strength of the guitar part that underpins it. It was reworked as 'Corkscrew' for the Steve Howe album *Turbulence*, and was all the better for it.

'Everybody's Song' (Anderson, Howe, Squire, White)
Source: Rhino re-master of *Tormato*
The instrumentation of 'Does It Really Happen' from *Drama* with a sketch of an entirely different song from Anderson placed over the top. It's interesting to hear what might have been, but the two parts don't really work together.

'Richard' (Anderson, Howe, Squire, Wakeman, White)
Source: *In A Word* boxed set
One of the era's better pieces, it actually sounds finished, if not particularly exciting, and it's not surprising that it didn't see the light of day until 2002.

'Crossfire' (Squire, Howe)
Source: *In A Word* boxed set
Presumably, an unused Howe / Squire / White trio piece from the *Drama* sessions, although it may be from Paris. Tonally, it's not really in keeping with the rest of the material on the album, but it's rather promising nonetheless.

Drama (1980)

Personnel:
Trevor Horn: vocals, bass
Chris Squire: bass, piano, vocals
Steve Howe: guitar, vocals
Alan White: drums, percussion, vocals
Geoff Downes: keyboards and vocoder
Arranged and produced by Yes. Backing tracks produced by Eddie Offord.
Recorded at the Town House, London, April to June 1980.
Engineer Hugh Padgham.
Mixed at Sarm Studios.
Highest chart places: UK: 2, USA: 18.
Running time: 36:55

The early part of 1980 was another period of crisis for Yes. With the Paris Sessions of late 1979 suspended the plan was that they would reconvene in the new year in London, when Alan White's foot injury had healed. This was a messy break-up, with Wakeman and Anderson not engaging in attempts to entice them back to London. Whether the pair formally left the band is open to interpretation. In his autobiography, Steve Howe reports that Anderson did show up at the studio at one point and played the band some of the songs he had been working on. They were full of cheery choruses and major keys – indeed, much of Anderson's solo album *Song of Seven*, released later that year, consists of such songs, so Howe's comment rings true. Wakeman never showed at all.

As a result, with White now recovered, the three remaining members continued to rehearse. Having the same management – Brian Lane – the Buggles were introduced to the band, consisting of Trevor Horn and Geoff Downes, who had had a massive UK hit in 1979 with their bubblegum novelty-pop classic 'Video Killed the Radio Star'. This had given them some fame, and their debut album, *The Age of Plastic,* also contained some great songs amongst the futuristic techno-sheen.

To some, the collaboration (unkindly called 'Yuggles' by the nay-sayers) was a joke. A ridiculous meeting of old-school progressive gravitas and lightweight pop. Others, however, saw the truth of the matter. These were proper musicians with the right credentials and attitude. Hadn't people seen Downes's keyboard rig in the 'Video Killed the Radio Star' video? He was clearly a prog fan at heart, even if he did play in rubber gloves – in a Buggles video, at least. That Horn was a fine, talented musician and sang in a similar register to Jon Anderson was also helpful. Their introductory piece, 'We Can Fly From Here', was – and remains – a terrific song, although it failed to make it onto the resulting album, the band opting instead for their more collaborative pieces. However, they did pick apart a new Horn/Downes song, 'I am a Camera' for the terrific epic 'Into the Lens'.

With the new Yes in place, the path of the album did not run completely smoothly, with Eddie Offord arriving to produce, then departing again fairly quickly, his eccentricity too much for everyone.

This is a typical Yes move. When in crisis, the band returns to the mean. In this case, it meant hiring Eddie, the man so responsible for the success of everything from *The Yes Album* to *Relayer,* while the album also saw the first Roger Dean cover on a studio album since *Relayer*, even if it (arguably) wasn't his finest work. With a (supposedly sell-out) tour booked for later in the year, the new band worked long hours to get the finished album complete by June, with Steve Howe recording his guitars without the band at RAK Studios. Trevor Horn even got married, spending a weekend in Bournemouth rather than the exotic two-week honeymoon planned. But they got there.

The resulting album did well commercially, reaching number two in Britain. Critics seemed to like it, too. It remains a band favourite, and after some hostility from fans to the line up at the time, seems to have settled into a favourite with many supporters as well. Considering the chaos and speed with which the album was created, it is a remarkably powerful and cohesive effort. The 'power trio' of Howe, Squire and White are on stupendous form, seemingly unshackled once again by commercial considerations. Howe, in particular, is remarkable and with the battle between guitar and keyboards settled – Downes defers – he is allowed the space to produce his best work since Relayer. Horn fits in very well – on album at least – providing just enough Anderson-ness to provide comfort but also plenty of his own personality. There are just hints of the popular genres at the time – heavy metal and new wave – but fundamentally, this is a great, powerful progressive rock album.

The eventful *Drama* tour saw Horn struggle with the Anderson material when tired and also receive a somewhat hostile reception from a small minority of the audiences in the UK. The album had been somewhat repressed until the Benoît David / Jon Davidson era when 'Machine Messiah' and 'Tempus Fugit' were reintroduced into the set, culminating in full-album renditions during 2017 and 2018.

'Machine Messiah' (Horn, Downes, Squire, Howe, White)
Falsely accused of being 'heavy metal' on release by a press hungry to associate Yes with the current trends, to wit the 'New Wave of British Heavy Metal', this superb piece does start with a heavy section, brought about by its deliberate, ponderous tone and White's powerful drumming, more than overdriven guitars. Indeed, the verse has a lightness of touch and energy – not to mention a wonderful soaring guitar melody from Howe, plus some neo-classical organ and a synthesiser solo – all within the first four and a half minutes. This is all very Yes so far. Whether by intent or design, the band also introduce Horn as lead vocalist gradually, with Squire very prominent in the opening salvos. Only during the atmospheric acoustic section do we realise:

'Yes have a new singer and he's actually ok!' 'Machine Messiah', written by the ensemble as a band pretty quickly, is a complete triumph. It offers no agenda – it isn't trying to shock (like 'Sound Chaser') or follow fashion (like 'Arriving UFO'); it looks back to *Fragile* and offers up a piece of well-structured, beautifully played progressive rock.

'Machine Messiah' was played on the *Drama* tour, but as you would expect, it was dropped when Anderson returned to the fold. When Benoît David was recruited in 2008, the band felt the freedom to place it back in the set again, and it went on to become the centrepiece of the set when *Drama* as played in its entirety in 2017.

'White Car' (Horn, Downes, Squire, Howe, White)
Played mainly by Downes on the Fairlight keyboard, but with added instrumentation from Howe and White, this short piece is actually very effective as a pallet cleanser after the bombast of 'Machine Messiah'. On the night I saw the band in London in 1980, it was played as an *a capella* piece at the end of the set as a tribute to the John Lennon, who had just been murdered.

'Does It Really Happen?' (Horn, Downes, Squire, Howe, White)
One of the tracks that the band were working on in Paris before Christmas, this version gives the piece a makeover and shows that the band could still play with some complexity, with Squire, in particular, holding the piece together with some astonishing bass playing. Howe mainly plays rhythm here, with Downes given the opportunity to shine on organ and synthesiser during the coda, (definitely shades of Asia here), which also includes a proper bass solo from Squire. White also shows off his mallet-percussion skills with what sounds like some nifty marimba.

'Into the Lens' (Horn, Downes, Squire, Howe, White)
This second proper 'epic' adapts the Buggles song 'I Am A Camera' and extends it in the Yes style. With choral voices the main vocal tool on the first half of the album, the verses here give Horn his first extensive lead vocal. The 'and you, may find time will blind you' section, with Horn and Squire singing in harmony – is spine-tingling and the whole piece is relentless – progressive rock played with the intensity of metal, with Howe soloing his heart out on both Fender Telecaster and his trusty pedal steel. One issue caused some Yes fans to baulk a little, namely the 'I am a Camera' hook, which some found too poppy to be Yes, even worse when played on the Vocoder – but we all soon got over it. Another terrific piece of music, beautifully constructed and executed.

'Run Through the Light' (Horn, Downes, Squire, Howe, White)
Probably the song that played most with what Yes were – or could be – this piece has Horn playing fretless bass at Squire's insistence, one of only two times another musician has played bass on a Yes track, the other being Billy Sherwood

on 'The More We Live, let Go'. His very different style is very impressive here
on a song that owes a great deal – in this version at least – to the Police and the
pop-reggae so popular around this time. Not that there's reggae here exactly,
but the band certainly have fun with some rather more modern stylings – a
complete album sounding like this might have been interesting (if unlikely) had
the line up ventured back into the studio. The finished version is certainly an
improvement on the first attempt recorded during The Paris Sessions, and the
closing instrumental section is inspired, fading out too early.

'Tempus Fugit' (Horn, Downes, Squire, Howe, White)
The album finishes superbly with this powerful piece, based around Squire's
harmonised bass line – one of his finest – played lightening fast. But there's
more than bass to this astonishing, breathless five minutes. Each musician
gels with each other while Downes' vocoder reminds us – triumphantly –
which band we are listening to. This was the other piece re-introduced to
the live set in the late 2000s, albeit played at a slightly less breakneck pace.
Trevor Horn also chose this song to play when he guested with the band
in 2016 and 2018, a bold choice considering how breathless a piece it is. A
superb close to a great album.

Related tracks
'Have We Really Got to Go through This'. (Howe, Squire, White)
Source: The Rhino reissue of *Drama*.
This is an up-tempo song – some might almost consider it simple – with a
distinct punk / new wave vibe. It was an instrumental piece that the trio were
working on prior to the arrival of Horn and Downes.

'Go Through This' (live)
Source: *The Word Is Live* boxed set
The piece above was finally worked into a full track and was played live on
some dates of the *Drama* tour as a short, punky pop song. The rough version
on the *Word is Live* boxed set does it few favours, but you do get the gist.

'We Can Fly From Here' (Horn, Downes)
Source: *The Word Is Live* boxed set
We will talk about the song that Downes and Howe used as their calling card
in a later chapter, but the only contemporary version by Yes is the live one on
The Word Is Live, which shows how little it was tampered with when it was
finally released in 2011.

'Song No. 4 (Satellite)' (Howe, Squire, White)
Source: The Rhino reissue of *Drama*.
Another piece being worked on by the trio, it was never developed with
Horn and Downes and so remains a promising backing track as far as Yes

are concerned, although it was reworked as the song provisionally called 'Telephone Secrets' when Squire and White played with Jimmy Page in the short-lived XYZ project when Yes dissolved after the *Drama* tour.

'I Am A Camera' (Horn, Downes)
Source: The Buggles album *Adventures in Modern Recording*.
The bare bones of 'Into the Lens' made it onto the Buggles second album, released in 1981, complete with drum machine, a lush, keyboard based arrangement and some great bass from Horn. It's very 'Buggles' and also rather good.

90125 (1983)

Personnel:
Jon Anderson: vocals Chris Squire: bass, vocals
Trevor Rabin: guitar, keyboards, vocals
Alan White: drums, percussion, Fairlight, vocals
Tony Kaye: keyboards
Deepak Khazanchi: sitar and tambura on 'It Can Happen'
Graham Preskett: violin on 'Leave It'
Trevor Horn: backing vocals
Produced at Sarm Studios, London, by Trevor Horn
Julian Mendelson: additional engineer
Stuart Bruce: additional engineer
Jonathan Jeczalik: keyboard programming
Dave Lawson: keyboard programming
Keith Finney: assistant engineer
Recording dates: November 1982 to July 1983
Released November 1983.
Highest chart places: UK: 16, USA: 5
Running time: 44:49

At the end of the *Drama* tour in 1980, Yes were seemingly over as a band.
Steve Howe and Geoff Downes formed Asia, Trevor Horn restarted his
production career and Chris Squire and Alan White spent some months
rehearsing a band with Led Zeppelin's Jimmy Page called XYZ (get it?). When
that project stalled in the face of management difficulties, the pair were
introduced to South African multi-instrumentalist Trevor Rabin. Rabin had
released three well-received solo albums while living in the UK at the end of
the 1970s but was now trying his luck in Los Angeles. The three gelled as a
unit, and when Squire recruited Tony Kaye after a meeting socially, the four-
piece band Cinema was born. For a while, at least.

The four rehearsed hard and began an album with Trevor Horn producing
at Sarm Studios towards the end of 1982.

Recording went well, although Horn and Kaye did not see eye to eye, and
within a few weeks, the keyboard player was back in Los Angeles. As he
points out in his autobiography, it was never Horn's intention to fire Kaye
from the band, just from the session. This left Rabin to fill the gaps.

Furthermore, with Rabin and Squire slated to share lead vocal duties, there
was some record company concern that the band was not strong enough
in the vocal department. Atlantic label boss Phil Carson suggested Jon
Anderson as a possible singer, and despite some initial animosity between
him and Squire, he joined the project in the summer of 1983, fairly late in the
recording process. The band became Yes again.

Although it continues to have plenty of naysayers, *90125* is a really good
album. Despite the 1980s production bells and whistles, it stands up well

today. There are several reasons for this. Horn gave the band focus and concision, Rabin – as it turned out – was a first-rate musician and songwriter, albeit with a tendency to write and play within AOR conventions. As a result, the material is excellent throughout. The album has no filler, either; each track sounds fresh, different and well-crafted. But the thing that makes a good 'Cinema' album into a great Yes one is the sprinkling of fairy dust that Jon Anderson provides. His influence can be discerned by the number of writing credits he has – seven out of nine – amazing considering how late he was recruited to the project. His contributions take the album to another level.

It is likely that Tony Kaye is rarely to be found in the final mix. He certainly plays on 'Cinema' and 'Hearts'. Seemigly out of the band completely, Kaye was replaced by Eddie Jobson (of UK, Frank Zappa and the early 1980s Jethro Tull). Indeed, Jobson can be seen briefly in the video for 'Owner of a Lonely Heart', and was involved in all the initial promotion for the album, although by the time the band were promoting the single, Kaye was back in the fold.

The timing, the good fortune of finding Anderson again, the huge success of 'Owner of a Lonely Heart' and this new corporate rock era led to a new lease of life for the band, which, after a huge world tour in 1984 and early 1985, they completely failed to capitalise upon.

'Owner of a Lonely Heart' (Rabin, Anderson, Squire, Horn)
There is no need to speculate a great deal about this most famous of tracks – a number one hit single in the USA, of course – since Trevor Rabin's original demo is in the public domain and many comments by Rabin – and Trevor Horn in particular – are available. The demo is remarkably faithful to the finished version, although the verses and intro are more orientated musically towards the AOR, which was Rabin's natural writing style. Horn heard the demo accidentally while Rabin was in the bathroom during a listening session and liked much of the song. Realising that the chorus, in particular, was a winner, he begged the band to record the track, feeling that the album needed a single, not just for the sake of sales, but for his own rapidly-burgeoning 'hit maker' reputation. He describes a process where the band rehearsed the song over the course of a week while he struggled to keep their 'rock' affectations out of their arrangement. He rewrote the verses with Rabin, making them more concise, but allowed Jon Anderson to rewrite some of the words to the second verse. The gunshot after the 'eagle in the sky' lyric is Horn 'literally' shooting down the eagle. The famous Synclavier orchestral stabs were added post-recording BY Alan White, and the metronomic beat is provided not by programming alone but by manipulation of Alan White's snare drum, tuned to a top A.

'Owner of a Lonely Heart' is the first track to demonstrate one of the main features of the Rabin-era Yes albums – the contrast between the voices of Rabin and Anderson. Rabin has the smooth, AOR tones, while Anderson's schoolboy alto has more attack, and his delivery of the lead vocal here is the icing on the cake, lifting the song from the good to the great. Rabin's innovative guitar solo also impresses, with its use of a harmonizer pedal playing fifths, as does a nifty key change just before the fade out. It was also a bold move to open the album with the track, very much a statement that this was a 'new' Yes.

Despite a couple of pretty terrible videos – readers might like to check out the alternative 'desert set' video on Youtube to the more often seen 'dramatic'version – the quality of the song and Horn's remarkable production lifted it into the top twenty in nineteen different territories. Only in the unforgiving UK market – where Yes were as unfashionable as a band could possibly be – did it disappoint, reaching number 28. So iconic has the song become, however, that it has had the remix treatment several times, most famously by Max Graham who had a UK top ten hit with the track in 2012.

'Hold On' (Rabin, Anderson, Squire)
'Hold On' is a big, cinematic, melodic rock song in the Rabin AOR style with a lead vocal from Anderson. It became a live favourite on tour, and although the song itself is relatively conventional, the beat – with its lovely 'swing' and the vocal arrangements throughout – lifts the track from the ordinary and gives plenty of hints of 1970s Yes alongside Rabin's neo-metal riffing.

'It Can Happen' (Squire, Anderson, Rabin)
Another track that benefited from fairly extensive reworking after Anderson came on board, 'It Can Happen' was restructured to cut out a mediocre verse originally sung by Squire. After an interesting intro played by Deepak Khazanchi on sitar, the replacement verse – the 'constant fight' section – is much better, making excellent use of some heavy reverb on the piano, and some inspired, heavily-treated backing vocals from Squire. The verse builds tension – released in the chorus – which remains from the Cinema version, which is also available on the Rhino re-master and the *Yesyears* compilation. The spoken word section during the guitar solo is from *The Importance of Being Earnest* by Oscar Wilde.

'Changes' (Rabin, Anderson, White)
'Changes' was instantly my favourite song on the album when it was released in 1983, perhaps because it seemed both immediate and progressive. The powerful mallet-percussion and bass intro – written by White – also includes some interesting eastern-style guitar before Rabin's bold, shredded guitar introduces the main song, with the riff now played on piano. The way that the drums and the guitar seem to weave around each other in this section is also inspired and then – all of a sudden – we are in 4/4 and Rabin is bringing things down to sing us a standard tale of love lost. The chorus – sung in harmony by Anderson and Squire – is catchy, and the contrast between

these sections and the parts sung by Rabin is nicely done. Although the song has a conventional middle eight – sung by Rabin – this section also has an unconventional middle eight with Anderson's gentle 'one word from you' section, which he probably wrote, adding a nice lyrical twist to the song, and which builds tension before the release of the final chorus and a final return to White's opening.

'Changes' represents all that is good about Rabin era Yes. It is a modern, conventional hard rock song given a bold 'Yes' treatment. It works beautifully and has rightly become a classic.

'Cinema' (Squire, Rabin, White, Kaye)
Credited to all four musicians, this thrilling but brief instrumental was recorded live at Air Studios. White and Squire are particularly impressive here, although White's crash cymbal 'splashes' might have been toned down in the mix. Apparently, this was supposed to be the opening to a twenty-minute progressive rock epic called 'Time'. In 1982! The mind boggles. The piece won a Grammy for 'Best Instrumental' in 1983.

'Leave It' (Squire, Rabin, Horn)
The second single from the album, this track was originally conceived as an *a capella* piece before some basic band instrumentation was added. It is a masterpiece of vocal processing, with Rabin and Squire laying down vocal track after track to Horn's masterly direction. Anderson's brief (but useful) contributions were added much later. It has an insistent keyboard and bass riff and a pleasing, sing-song melody, but the 80s stylings feel rather more forced than on 'Owner of a Lonely Heart'. It still stands up to repeated listens, however. The single mix is only subtly different to the album version, and an *a capella* version was also released.

'Our Song' (Anderson, Squire, Rabin, White, Kaye)
Though it is largely conventional in structure, there is an up-tempo exuberance to this track that always satisfies. Anderson sings the lead vocal, and there are very few bells and whistles production-wise, giving it a real 'band' feel. The keyboards – possibly played by Kaye as he has a writing credit – are some of the best on the album, too.

'City of Love' (Rabin, Anderson)
'City of Love' is Yes's heaviest track at time of writing (in 2023). Clearly, this was very much Rabin's show, with a tone similar to his solo albums, although giving the lead vocal to Anderson – who delivers a rasping vocal performance rarely heard outside live shows – is something of a masterstroke. Despite the deliberately plodding beat, there is actually more complexity to the arrangement than might first be apparent, and the vocal arrangement – mainly layered up by Rabin – is once again excellent, as is White's thunderous

drumming. The guitar solo is an exercise in flashy feedback manipulation, extended to become a showcase for Rabin's virtuosity at live shows.

'Hearts' (Anderson, Squire, Rabin, White, Kaye)
I will admit to being largely unconvinced by the progressive epics in the Rabin- era Yes albums, and to me, 'Hearts' is a little lacklustre. That said, there's still a lot to enjoy. Anderson clearly had a strong hand in the finalisation of this piece, and it is unclear how much work had been done on it before his arrival. He dominates, and in particular, many of the backing vocals are his too, whereas, on the main bulk of the album, it is Squire and Rabin that provide them, as they do towards the end of the song here. His voice contrasts well with Rabin in the gentle opening, although I find the middle instrumental section a little lacking in inspiration. The main vocal theme is pretty enough, and the hard rocking section – with some swirling Hammond from Kaye – is very good, but to me, overall, it is a slightly disappointing ending, just a little too sentimental to my ears. To others, however, it is a classic.

The band played it on the 1999 *Ladder* Tour (although it doesn't appear on the DVD) and Anderson has played it in solo concerts from time to time, so this track clearly resonates beyond the Rabin era for Anderson, at least.

Related tracks
'Make It Easy' (Rabin)
This track is important for a couple of reasons. Firstly, it shows us how Cinema might have sounded. It is a decent Rabin song, sung by him in the AOR style, and feels like it might have been on one of his solo albums. The fusion-style intro, however, is better than the main song and was used by the band as the introduction to 'Owner of a Lonely Heart', when the Rabin line-ups played it between 1984 and 1994. Suffice to say, subsequent live lineups of the band have dropped it, although it reappeared on the Anderson, Rabin, Wakeman tours between 2016 and 2018.

'It's Over' (Rabin)
This is another decent Rabin song, very well played by the band but very much in his solo style. It is particularly notable for his rather strained lead vocal, fairly typical of his early solo albums. The chorus is concise and has echoes of Queen in its operatic vocal arrangement. It might have made the cut on many rock band's albums, but on *90125,* this song would have been out of place as presented here.

'Owner of a Lonely Heart' (extended remix)
A staple part of any single release in the 80s was the twelve-inch version, and this remix was just that. These remixes fell into two camps – either an enhancement and extension of the main song or an impressionistic dance

version, with hardly any melodic relationship to its parent track. Sadly, this falls into the latter category, and as such is hard to listen to outside a club setting. A similar remix of 'Leave It' exists, though only on the twelve-inch single of that song.

Big Generator (1987)

Personnel:
Jon Anderson: vocals
Chris Squire: bass, vocals
Trevor Rabin: guitar, keyboards, vocals, string arrangements
Alan White: drums, percussion, vocals
Tony Kaye: Hammond organ and piano
James Zavala: horns on 'Almost Like Love' , harmonica on "Love Will Find a Way'
 Lee R. Thornburg: horns on 'Almost Like Love'
Nick Lane : horns on 'Almost Like Love'
Greg Smith: horns on 'Almost Like Love'
Produced by Yes, Trevor Horn, Trevor Rabin, Paul De Villiers
Recorded at Lark Studios, Italy; Sarm and Air studios, London and Southcombe, Westlake and Sunset Sound studios, Los Angeles, between 1985 and 1987.
Released September 1987
Highest Chart Positions: UK: 17, USA: 15
Running time: 43:48

With *90125* such a big hit, the resulting world tour, which mixed the new material with some Yes classics given a Rabin makeover, was also a huge success. Rabin couldn't have been more perfect for the 1980s version of Yes. Youngish, dashing, good looking but also immensely talented as a musician, he was able to handle Howe's parts – albeit reworked – with ease but also added some hard rocking style to the newer material. The tour was a big success artistically as well as commercially, although the 1980s style means that the footage – recorded on the very stylised *90125 Live* video – has not worn well. But the band played their socks off.

   Ending the tour at the start of 1985, what they should have done is produced a new album quickly, and had it out in early 1986 at the latest. What they actually did was lurch from studio to studio, getting very little done and spending huge amounts of money. The band recorded in Italy, to begin with. This was partially for tax reasons and partially because Rabin wanted the band to gel as a unit, with Trevor Horn again producing. Anderson's presence was not needed for the first few weeks, and when he got to Italy, he found partying and very little work. When these sessions produced very little, they switched to Sarm East and West in London, at which point Trevor Horn jumped ship, and the album was finished in Los Angeles with Rabin and Paul DeVilliers producing. There seems to have been a few power struggles, initially between Rabin and Horn, and also between Rabin and Anderson, over song-writing direction. In short,Yes went through the same sort of issues that many rock bands went through in the 1980s. There was too much money knocking around, and the band got locked into its own ego bubble – unable to see the bigger picture. After a tour to promote the album, which visited the USA and Japan but not Europe, Anderson decided to move on again.

In truth, you can hear the indecision in the final product. While most of the material is decent, there is a soullessness about the whole album that places a barrier between the listener and the band. Ironically, the shorter, more modern-sounding material on side one (of the vinyl) is the more impressive, while the two longer tracks on side two – 'I'm Running' and 'Final Eyes', although a little more progressive in spirit, lack intimacy. The fact that there are three songs on the album with 'love' in the title shows what the band were aiming at. After the immediacy of *90125,* Big Generator feels hugely overproduced with its layered backing vocals – with Squire's usually-distinctive vocals often buried – and over-busy instrumentation.

'The Rhythm of Love' (Kaye, Rabin, Anderson, Squire)
The first track of an album usually sets the tone of what is to follow, and it does here. It is a big, reverb-heavy rocker, albeit with some subtle touches in the middle eight. A minor hit as a single in the USA, reaching number 40, it has become the most-played song from the album in the live set over the years. The band even persuaded Howe to do a very creditable job playing it on the 2004 World Tour, and it represented the album when Anderson, Rabin and Wakeman played it on their 2017 and 2018 live dates. In the context of this 'new' version of Yes, it is very good indeed, although the 'love' it talks about here is 'carnal' rather than 'brotherly'. It was also played live on the *Big Generator* Tour as the set opener.

'Big Generator' (Rabin, Kaye, Anderson, Squire, White)
So to the title track, which mixes the orchestral 'stabs' from 'Owner' with the heaviest riffs yet heard on a Yes album (even if 'City of Love' remains the heaviest track). It balances a tense verse, sung by Anderson, with a chorus that contrasts high and low register vocals, dominated by Rabin. This is impressive stuff, the relative simplicity of the song contrasting with some interesting production techniques and some inventive, King Crimson-style guitar. The 'flying out the soft machine' section sounds like Godley and Creme, particularly some of the vocal techniques used on the *L* and *Freeze Frame* albums. It was played live on the *Big Generator* Tour.

'Shoot High, Aim Low' (White, Kaye, Rabin, Anderson, Squire)
Languid and quietly inventive, 'Shoot High, Aim Low' has some lovely acoustic guitar quite low in the mix, and – aside from the more obvious 'Changes' – has the best use of Anderson and Rabin sharing lead vocal duties. White's drum part was recorded in Italy, using the natural reverb available in the house they were staying in. The song takes its time to develop, with deftly-planted keyboards sweeping in and out of the mix. If the criticism that the album is 'over produced' can be levelled at it, then this song is the worst culprit, yet here it works. Unusual and powerful, it is probably the highlight of the album. It was played live on the *Big Generator* Tour.

'Almost Like Love' (Kaye, Rabin, Anderson, Squire)
I've always had a sneaking liking for this somewhat unsung track. It certainly rubbed a lot of Yes fans up the wrong way with its Motown-style drum pattern and – gasp – a horn section, playing the song's main riff. While it couldn't be any more different from the Yes of *Close to the Edge* it has an exuberance of its own. Anderson delivers one of his part-scat / part-raps, there's some great Hammond from Kaye and a speedy guitar solo from Rabin. Hardly a classic, but as an old-fashioned up-tempo closer to side one of the vinyl version, it's rather tasty. The song was played as the set opener on the 1987 leg of the *Big Generator* tour but was dropped in favour of *Rhythm of Love* in 1988.

'Love Will Find A Way' (Rabin)
A string quartet introduces this Rabin pop/rock song, originally written for Stevie Nicks. It has an infectious sing-along quality, and it is not hard to see it as a big hit for Nicks. For Yes, it was a minor one, reaching number 30 in the USA and 73 in the UK. While Rabin is the lead vocalist, Anderson and Squire both make good contributions, and there are short solos for Kaye and James Zavala, who plays harmonica (not Squire, as some listeners assume!). It was played live on the *Big Generator* Tour.

'Final Eyes' (Rabin, Kaye, Anderson, Squire)
This longer piece, sung by Anderson – with help on some lines from Rabin – feels like an attempt to recapture the magic of the 70s version of the band. Rabin's guitar actually sounds like Steve Howe until he cranks up the overdrive halfway through, and there are some nostalgic Hammond whirls from Kaye. That said, I find the song unconvincing, perhaps a little too sweet and sentimental in both melody and lyric to feel like 'old' Yes. There are three songs with 'love' in the title on the album, and while 'Final Eyes' isn't one of them, it is the most syrupy of the lot.

'I'm Running' (Rabin, Squire, Anderson, Kaye, White)
Rather better, but still not quite up there with the band's best work, is 'I'm Running'. Squire's terrific bass riff – with treble turned up to the max – introduces the piece, a difficult opening, leading into the main verse, with its chanted chorus. This is by far the most progressive piece on the album, albeit awash with 80s production techniques, with piano – possibly played by Rabin in effect-laden form – and Kaye's organ heavily featured. This is a piece worthy of further examination, and it would certainly be interesting if Rabin-orientated lineups at least had a stab at playing this track live in the future.

'Holy Lamb (Song for Harmonic Convergence)' (Anderson)
The sort of Anderson piece that he loves to close albums with, this song is throw-away stuff, and belongs on a solo record rather than a Yes album.

Here, it feels underdeveloped and something of an afterthought, perhaps an attempt to keep Anderson happy on an album he felt he had not contributed enough to. It didn't work and nor does the track. It was, however, played live on the *Big Generator* Tour.

Related tracks

There are no related songs from this era, although the 2009 reissue does include various contemporary remixes of 'Love Will Find a Way' and 'The Rhythm of Love'.

Anderson, Bruford, Wakeman, Howe (1989)

Personnel:
Jon Anderson: Vocals Steve Howe: Guitars
Rick Wakeman: Keyboards
Bill Bruford: Electronic and Acoustic Drums
Tony Levin: Bass, Stick, Vocals
Matt Clifford: Keyboards, Programming, Orchestration, Vocals
Milton McDonald: Rhythm Guitar
Backing vocals: The Oxford Circus Singers – Deborah Anderson, Tessa Niles,
Carol Kenyon, Francis Dunnery.
JMC Singers: Jon Anderson, Matt Clifford, Chris Kimsey. Emerald Community
Singers, Monserrat.
Produced by Chris Kimsey and Jon Anderson at Air Studios, Monserrat and Air
Studios, London.
Pre-production recording at Studio La Frette, Paris.
Released: 20 June 1989
Highest chart places: UK: 14, USA: 30
Running time: 59:05

Yes, I know. This is not a Yes album, and as a result, not part of the
'catalogue'. However, so crucial is it to the fate of the band over the next
few years of its turbulent existence, that I have taken a little poetic licence
– for one album only – and included it. Some people will consider this an
'honorary' Yes album anyway, as I do. Others will be vehemently opposed
– many Yes fans love to be vehemently opposed to things – but I hope they
will, at least understand my logic, and bear with me.

Yes albums have been created in many ways. Although most often
collaborative, if not always democratic, sometimes the impetus has come
from one or a group of musicians, with others falling in line – *Open Your
Eyes* would be a good example. In the case of *Anderson, Bruford, Wakeman,
Howe* the impetus came from a frustrated Jon Anderson, who had suffered
several years as – seemingly – a bit part player in his own movie. He had
recorded a solo album, *In the City of Angels,* released in the spring of 1988,
which had failed to trouble any charts, despite its commercial leanings. With
the support of his wife Jennifer, who felt that it was time for 70s style Yes
to make a return, he decided that he wanted a band, and he knew some
musicians that might be interested ...

Anderson had not played with – or had any real contact with – Howe
for ten years. He had not played with Bruford since 1972, but Howe had
used Bruford as a session player on a few occasions. Anderson had also
become firm friends with Wakeman, but they hadn't played together since
his appearance on Wakeman's 1981 solo album *1984*. In this case, all were
recruited separately and based on one-to-one conversations with the trio, who
all supplied material, particularly Howe – he formed a temporary band based

around keyboard player Matt Clifford and guitarist Milton McDonald to create demos in a studio in Paris.

Then Wakeman and Bruford joined Anderson at George Martin's Air Studios in Montserrat to record the album. Howe chose not to go, recording his guitars on his own in London. Initially, Anderson had hoped that Squire would join the project at some point, but with Bruford preferring not to work with him, the drummer suggested his former King Crimson cohort Tony Levin, who did a sterling job. Experienced producer Chris Kimsey – best know to progressive rock fans for his work with Marillion – was brought in by new record company Arista, nervous about allowing Anderson too much freedom.

The resulting album was well received and sold well for Arista, certified gold in the USA. What is old style Yes? Had the band achieved what it wanted? Yes and no. There are aspects of the album that really work; it certainly has energy and commitment from all the players. There are hints of what the Bruford-era band might have sounded like had it stayed together beyond 1972, and also what the *Tormato* lineup might have produced had it fought its way past its differences. Bruford's electronic drums – in particular – create a tone unlike anything ever heard before on a Yes project, even if those sounds have dated badly. Furthermore, I really miss the intricacy of Bruford's acoustic playing; his textures on this album are in the sounds he creates, not his actual technique.

Also somewhat dated are some of Wakeman's keyboard textures, although one of the delights of the album is the huge amount of piano on it. Yet I can never quite escape the feeling that what I am listening to is an enhanced Jon Anderson solo album. Musically, it goes in places that, I suspect, Squire would never have allowed, and as a result, feels like an album with various aspects of the Yes sound, rather than an album that is awash with it. Nonetheless, as a possible 'Yes' in an alternative universe, it is as valid as any of the 'fringe' albums, like *Fly From Here* or even *Big Generator*.

The project really became a 'band' on the long world tour of 1989, which saw them mixing up material from the album with Bruford-era Yes classics. Again, these shows felt different, tonally, from the standard Yes shows, with a different structure, especially each band member introducing himself with a solo spot at the start of each show. The live renditions of, for instance, 'Close to the Edge' are full of precision, commitment and power. Seemingly with good album sales and a massively successful tour, against the run of fashion, the future was rosy and the band would continue as a more collaborative venture. Or would it?

'Themes (Sound / Second Attention / Soul Warrior)' (Anderson, Bruford, Wakeman, Howe)
This is a strong start, Wakeman's introduction – played on piano and synthesiser – is very impressive, although as soon as Bruford's electronic

drums enter, we know we are in the 1980s. It's a powerful opening, given something of a Yes vibe with Howe's lead work and Wakeman's jaunty synthesiser soloing. The 'Soul Warrior' section, again, suggests a version of Yes that is absorbing new styles and sounds. No Yes album ever sounded quite like this. Overall, 'Themes' is an excellent beginning, and was included in the subsequent tour.

'Fist of Fire' (Anderson, Bruford, Wakeman, Howe)
The momentum is maintained by this exuberant short piece. Like 'Themes', Anderson's vocal is percussive, even aggressive and Bruford's electronic percussion really works here. However, the star is Wakeman, swamping the track with thrilling Minimoog solos over a rich poly-synthesiser backing, while Howe also embellishes impressively. It is perfection in 3.32 minutes. An alternative mix of the track, which features a lot more guitar, was included on the *In A Word* box set. In truth, I prefer the original. Howe, recording on his own, played a lot more guitars than are heard on the final mix of the album, and was (understandably, in a sense) somewhat aggrieved to find a fair amount of what he recorded on the cutting room floor. However, the restored guitars in the alternative version are just too intrusive to be effective.

'Brother of Mine (The Big Dream / Nothing Can Come Between Us / Long Lost Brother Of Mine)' (Anderson, Bruford, Wakeman, Howe, Geoff Downes)
Despite being the longest piece on the album, I have never been particularly impressed by this track, which feels like three decent, but non-essential songs strung together. 'The Big Dream' and 'Nothing Can Come Between Us' sections definitely have the 'Anderson solo track' feel, although Howe and Wakeman's contributions are impressive, the latter on (digital-sounding) piano. The final section, mainly written by Howe with Geoff Downes, is catchy and again, Howe and Wakeman make excellent contributions without getting in each other's way. However, except for the final few bars, the instrumentation is embellishment rather than a major part of the piece, and the songs dominate, for better or worse. Released as a single in the UK, a very short and a longer edit of the track can be found on disc two of the 2014 Esoteric re-issue. The piece was played live on the subsequent tour and a glossy promotional video was recorded for it.

'Birthright' (Anderson, Bruford, Wakeman, Howe, Max Bacon)
Howe's classical guitar comes into its own on this superb track, co written with his GTR band member Max Bacon, with lyrics about the murderous nuclear testing by the British in Woomera, Australia. This is a fantastically atmospheric piece of music, which also makes the best of Wakeman's keyboard parts toward the end of the song, propelled by Bruford's tribal drumming. At just over six minutes, it is the perfect length to tell its story.

Again, this was played live on the subsequent tour, and proved something of ashow-stopperr.

'The Meeting' (Anderson, Bruford, Wakeman, Howe)
Despite the writing credit, this lovely piano and vocal piece has 'Anderson / Wakeman' written all over it. It features one of Wakeman's prettier piano pieces and a typical Anderson melody. It is the only piece from the album that has had any sort of life beyond the life of the band, played as it was as part of the acoustic set on the 2004 Yes World Tour, and deservedly so, as it's lovely.

'Quartet (I Wanna Learn / She Gives me Love / Who was The First / I'm Alive)' (Anderson, Bruford, Wakeman, Howe, Ben Dowling)
It would be wrong to suggest that the album goes off the rails at this point, but the next two pieces are wafer-thin. Both 'Quartet' and 'Teakbois' are perfectly pleasant but so dominated by somewhat cloying Anderson-penned songs that they waste the musicians playing them. Howe's guitar beginning 'Quartet' is beautiful and Wakeman plays some lovely trumpet-style synthesiser, but this feels more like a Jon and Vangelis track without the invention to the arrangement that Vangelis might bring. The piece also has a false ending before the 'I'm Alive' section, making it feel like a separate track entirely. Overall, 'Quartet' is pleasant enough, but is a rather odd and unsatisfying listen.

'Teakbois' (Anderson, Bruford, Wakeman, Howe)
Something of a 'marmite' track – you either love it or hate it – this piece, clearly inspired by the band's Monserrat location – would never have made it to a Yes album. It's exuberant and fun, and Wakeman is clearly enjoying himself, peeling off various West Indian-inspired solos. I rather like it, I have to admit, and the song should really not be taken too seriously – it's very light-hearted but again, wafer-thin. The massed vocalists later in the song foreshadow the next track by singing a snatch of the main theme.

'Order of the Universe (Order Theme / Rock Gives Courage / It's So Hard To Grow / The Order Of The Universe)'(Anderson, Bruford, Wakeman, Howe, Rhett Lawrence)
And so to the big finish. This is a very impressive piece, full of grandeur and – after the lightness of the two tracks before it – it rocks pretty hard, too. The theme – played by Wakeman on synthesiser is powerful, but Howe's spine-tingling guitar makes the track, before Anderson's rock vocal on 'Rock Gives Courage'. This is somewhat obvious stuff, but we'll allow the band a little rock and roll posturing – it was the 80s, after all. If anything, 'It's So Hard To Grow' rocks even harder, before the choral 'Order Of The Universe' hook starts to invade the track. There is some great soloing by Howe – criminally

low in the mix – a brief, somewhat dated percussion break, then a reprisal of the theme and the track ends with a flurry of percussion. This piece was, understandably, a centrepiece of the live set on the subsequent tour. 'Rock Gives Courage' was written by Anderson with Rhett Lawrence, presumably during the writing sessions for *In The City Of Angels*, Anderson's 1988 solo album.

'Let's Pretend' (Anderson, Bruford, Wakeman, Howe, Vangelis)
This lovely closing piece is dominated by Howe's classical guitar and a simple, heartfelt vocal from Anderson with just a touch of synthesiser from Wakeman. It was a result of Anderson's writing sessions with Vangelis the year before, and it's a charming end to the album.

Related tracks
'Vultures In The City' (Anderson, Bruford, Wakeman, Howe)
A rather slight but atmospheric song, with some nice slide guitar from Howe. It was released as the B side to 'Brother Of Mine'.

Union (1990)

Personnel:
Jon Anderson: vocals
Chris Squire: bass, vocals
Steve Howe: guitars, vocals
Trevor Rabin: guitars, keyboards, vocals
Tony Kaye: keyboards
Rick Wakeman: Keyboards Alan White: drums, percussion
Bill Bruford: electronic and Acoustic Drums, Percussion
Tony Levin: bass
Jimmy Haun: guitar
Billy Sherwood: vocals and other instruments (uncredited)
Produced by Jonathan Elias, Steve Howe, Mark Mancina, Eddie Offord, Billy
Sherwood. Associate Producer: Jon Anderson
Recorded: 1989 to 1991
Released: 20 April 1991
Highest chart places: UK: 7, USA: 15
Running time: 65:23 (standard international CD)

If ever there was an album in the Yes catalogue that typifies the continual
infighting and management difficulties over the years, it is the *Union* album.
This now seems like an ironic title. In 1990 it was considered anything but.

Anderson, Bruford, Wakeman, Howe – having come off the road – were
due to start work on a new album while Yes still technically existed as
the remains of the band that had recorded *Big Generator*. Once again, Jon
Anderson seems to have been the bridge between the two camps, and with
Arista (the ABWH label) after a hit, it seemed that Trevor Rabin's pen might
be able to provide that. From that, a sort of artificial amalgamation of the
two bands seemed to have been worked out, with Anderson singing on the
four tracks recorded by the Rabin, Squire, White and Kaye version, and Chris
Squire adding vocals to a few of the ABWH tracks.

In a revealing interview with Henry Potts, Jonathan Elias, the producer
of the ABWH tracks, paints a picture of a band with almost no material
attempting to piece an album together as the age-old antagonisms were
beginning to emerge, mainly between Anderson and Howe and Howe and
Wakeman. He describes Anderson and Howe refusing to be in the studio
together and Wakeman and Howe refusing to listen to each other's parts,
leading to arrangement issues as had been the case on *Tormato*. In the end,
Anderson took control of the situation and a host of session players were
used – mainly for keyboard parts, but also Jimmy Haun to play some of
Steve Howe's guitar parts. These decisions were not well received by either
musician, as you can imagine.

Union is not the worst album in the Yes catalogue. It actually has some
excellent tracks. However, it has no cohesion as a record and many of the

ABWH tracks feel underdeveloped. Even despite that, it's much too long. With the addition of the rather good 'Give and Take' on the European CD edition, the album comes in at almost 70 minutes and at least five of the ABWH tracks could have been lost without making the album any weaker. It's all a bit of a mess, but when it's good – it's very good. The main problem with it is that, after a fairly strong start, the album peters out with no climactic track to lift the heart. The final few pieces of music may just be the least listened to in Yes history.

On the back of the success of ABWH, and with some not-inconsiderable buzz based around the re-union of all eight musicians, the album did quite well commercially, making the top ten in the UK, but with some poor reviews, the success was not sustained. The subsequent tour, however, was a considerable success, with the eight-piece band playing arenas in the round, as the band had done in 1978-1979. Wakeman, in particular, really enjoyed it, striking up an unlikely life-long friendship with the softly-spoken Rabin, and while there was some tension between Rabin and Howe, the contrast between White (playing acoustic drums) and Bruford (inventive on his electronic kit) also worked nicely.

'I Would Have Waited Forever' (Anderson, Howe, Jonathan Elias)
Production: Jonathan Elias. Additional vocals: Chris Squire
This is a strong opening, setting out the 'tone' of the tracks recorded by the ABWH faction – hard-ish rock with some progressive and pop twists. Indeed, of all the Yes albums, it is ironic that this is the one that sounds most like Asia. Howe (presumably) delivers a catchy riff and Squire's backing vocals are really effective, although the rhythm guitar sounds like it might be Jimmy Haun. To begin the track with Anderson's catchy vocal hook is also a minor masterstroke. It packs a lot into six and a half minutes, and frustratingly seems to be going somewhere interesting just as it fades out. Nonetheless, it is a decent start.

'Shock To The System' (Anderson, Howe, Elias)
Production: Jonathan Elias.
The momentum continues with another strong track, this time a slice of hard rock with more strong work from Howe (and possibly Haun), and another big riff providing the backbone, even if Anderson's vocal melody betrays a softer edge. This track was rehearsed and played by all eight members of the band early in the set on the *Union* tour, particularly as it is well suited to Rabin's style as well as Howe's.

'Masquerade' (Howe)
Production: Steve Howe
There's a history – perhaps even a tradition – of Howe solo pieces on Yes albums, of course, so there's no shame in this track at all, particularly as it's

a lovely piece – one of Howe's finest. It was nominated for a Grammy Award, and deservedly so. However, what it's doing sequenced third on a full band album is another matter. A rather odd decision, but a lovely track.

'Lift Me Up' (Rabin, Squire)
Production: Trevor Rabin. Programming: Mark Mancina.
We now switch to the Rabin / Squire version of the band, with this strong offering from Rabin, and a song which had originally been offered to the ABWH-version of the group, an idea which was abandoned as soon as the 'Union' idea was cooked up. It does demonstrate the contrived nature of some of the recording, however, with Anderson singing the first verse and then becoming buried in the backing vocal arrangement (if he is present at all), with Rabin taking over lead vocals thereafter. In terms of structure, it is fairly typical of Rabin's writing, a catchy pop song encased in a rather more progressive instrumental structure. The song was – understandably – released as a single, reaching number 86 in the USA, but spending six weeks at number one in the rock chart. As well as being played on the *Union* tour, and also the *Talk* tour, it was revived for the Yes – Featuring Anderson, Rabin, Wakeman tours in 2016 to 2018, so has had a longer life than most pieces from the album.

'Without Hope You Cannot Start The Day' (Anderson, Elias)
Production: Jonathan Elias. Guest vocals: Chris Squire
This maintains the tone of the previous ABWH tracks – a rather decent, gentle opening giving way to something rather more messy and unconvincing. Howe (assuming it's him) is impressive, Squire's vocals are again nicely integrated and – for the first time on the album – Wakeman can (probably) be heard, albeit low in the mix. Again it fades out just when it seems to be going somewhere, but overall the track feels cobbled together and might have been better off discarded.

'Saving My Heart' (Rabin)
Production: Trevor Rabin
This slice of Rabin-penned pop and cod-reggae is lightweight in the extreme, but at least holds together as a coherent song, making a better job of integrating Anderson into the mix. To be honest, though, as a piece of Yes music it's horrid. At least the ABWH tracks were trying to sound like Yes, this song sounds like it was written with other artists in mind, which it probably was. Be warned if you haven't played it in a while: it is annoyingly catchy.

'Miracle of Life' (Rabin, Mark Mancina)
Production: Trevor Rabin with Mark Mancina and Eddie Offord
From the ridiculous to the sublime. 'Miracle of Life', in this author's opinion, must go down as one of the unsung Yes classics (alongside 'To Be Over' and

'Dreamtime'), even if its organ riff is borrowed from Handel's Water Music. It takes the structure pioneered on 'Changes' from *90125* and makes it almost as good. Its exuberant and inspiring introduction features Alan White's best work on the album, while the superb main song sounds like Jon Anderson was born to sing it. If the band had had time to produce more pieces like this wonderful seven and a half minutes, then the album might have been as good as *90125*. As it is, it's frustrating that this standout piece of music should be surrounded by so much mediocrity.

'Silent Talking' (Anderson, Howe, Wakeman, Bruford, Elias)
Production: Jonathan Elias
At exactly four minutes long, this interesting track again shows what might have been. It has one of only two writing credits for Wakeman on the album and includes some parts that certainly sound like him. It also borrows a riff from 'Sensitive Chaos' that Howe would later use on his excellent solo album *Turbulence*. The track has two distinct parts – both excellent – which feel like they should have been sections of a longer piece, but here the song ends frustratingly quickly.

'The More We Live, Let Go' (Squire, Billy Sherwood)
Production: Eddie Offord and Billy Sherwood. Vocals, bass, guitar, keyboards: Billy Sherwood
As well as working with Rabin, Chris Squire was also developing a working friendship with Billy Sherwood, whose own relationship with the band would develop later. This slow-burn of a song is excellent, with Anderson again well integrated and sharing lead vocals with Squire and Sherwood. Sherwood also plays almost every instrument, even the bass part, which Squire liked enough from the demo to allow it to stay on the finished song. Given the relative homogeneity of the ABWH songs, this piece really stands out as something special.

'Angkor Wat' (Anderson, Wakeman, Elias)
Production: Jonathan Elias. Cambodian Poetry: Pauline Cheng
Left off the vinyl version of the album with some justification, this largely-ambient piece is somewhat forgettable, with some very dated keyboard sounds, and marks a real downturn in the album's fortunes. The subject matter deserved a better piece of music.

'Dangerous (Looking For The Light Of What You're Searching For)' (Anderson, Elias)
Production: Jonathan Elias. Featured guitar: Jimmy Haun. Guest vocals: Chris Squire
A slice of rather dumb pop / heavy rock, with funk overtones, this track was intended to capture the spirit of *90125*, but in fact, it gets caught up in its own late 80s / early 90s production style. It is only notable for some terrific

bass work from Tony Levin, his playing at last lifted from the stylistic shackles of being asked to sound like Chris Squire. Jimmy Haun is the featured guitarist; his playing is clearly very different from Howe's.

'Holding On' (Anderson, Elias, Howe)
Production: Jonathan Elias
This is the final 'full band' piece, a rather mediocre affair dominated by Anderson, with some decent work from Howe, Bruford and Levin and a short synthesiser solo from Wakeman (probably), but otherwise, the song is forgettable. It is another that might have been dropped to make the album more listenable as a whole. As the spiritual 'climax' of the whole recordit just isn't good enough.

'Evensong' (Bruford, Levin)
Production: Jonathan Elias
A short and charming instrumental for bass and electronic percussion that is completely wasted at the end of the album. If feels like a prologue to an epic that doesn't exist.

'Take The Water To The Mountain' (Anderson)
Production: Jonathan Elias
This is, let us not forget, the close of many versions of the CD – and of the vinyl version of the album. Again, it's a largely ambient piece with chanted vocals and electronic percussion very prominent. It's actually rather effective, but again as an album closer, it just doesn't work.

Related tracks
'Give And Take' (Anderson, Howe, Elias)
Production: Jonathan Elias
How ironic that one of the strongest ABWH tracks on the album should be missed off the vinyl and international versions completely. It's an exuberant, up-tempo piece, mercifully free of the production quirks that blight many of the ABWH songs. It makes some nice use of guitar harmonics and while some of the guitar may well be played by Haun, it's exciting and powerful without resorting to heavy rock histrionics. Anderson delivers his 'rock' voice very effectively. If you are outside the UK and have never heard this song, seek it out. It's a little gem.

'Love Conquers All' (Squire, Sherwood)
There are two versions of this Squire / Sherwood song in existence – one recorded during the *Union* sessions with lead guitar and lead vocals from Rabin and the other with Sherwood singing from the Squire / Sherwood *Conspiracy* album released at the end of the decade. The song itself is fine, if hardly earth-shattering, and the Rabin version is marginally the better of the two.

'The More We Live' (Squire, Sherwood)
A later version of the song from Union again from the Squire / Sherwood album *Conspiracy*. Anderson's voice is missed, but the production is smartened up considerably, making this – on balance – a more definitive version of the song, so worth seeking out.

Talk (1994)

Personnel:
Jon Anderson: lead and backing vocals
Chris Squire: bass guitar, backing vocals
Trevor Rabin: electric and acoustic guitars, keyboards, lead and backing vocals, programming
Alan White: drums
Tony Kaye: Hammond organ and piano
Produced, engineered and mixed by Trevor Rabin at the Jacaranda Room, Hollywood and A & M Studios, Hollywood
Engineering and mixing by Michael Jay
Recorded: 1992 and 1993
Released: March 1994
Highest chart places: UK: 20, USA: 33
Running time: 55:02

With all eight musicians that had played on the album taking part, the *Union* tour of 1991 was unique. From a spectator's point of view, it was an astonishing spectacle and musically very successful too. Despite this, there were tensions between Howe and Rabin and with Bruford always unlikely to continue with this sort of organisation, the band was left in limbo. Long-time Yes supporter at Atlantic, Phil Carson had formed a new label – Victory – and approached Trevor Rabin to produce a new Yes album. The new version of the band was to be a six-piece with Wakeman involved but without Howe. By the time pre-production began in 1993, Wakeman was out and – against all odds – the *90125* lineup was back in vogue.

But Rabin was more in tune with the needs of the lineup this time out, and actively sought the input of Anderson from the word go, with Squire less involved in the writing. Recording then began in Rabin's home studio at 'the Jacaranda Room' in California. Rabin was a pioneer of digital recording at the time, and *Talk* was one of the first albums to be recorded onto an Apple Macintosh rather than analogue tape, although the album took a fair while to record due to software issues. It was a common – somewhat ridiculous – misconception that it was recorded using synthetic instruments, when in fact, the album was recorded using conventional instruments, recorded to hard disc. As most will know, now almost all recording is done this way.

There is little doubt that the resulting album is a very classy recording. It sounds great, having lost the 1980s tricks and affectations that can be heard on *90125* or *Big Generator*, recording the instruments pretty much 'straight'.

Jon Anderson, as you might expect, sounds enthusiastic and invested in the material, and his vocals – particularly on the excellent 'State of Play' – are some of his most exuberant outside the 1970s. Tony Kaye, however, seems like a passenger once again, with Rabin playing most of the keyboards.

The album is, however, a very song-orientated, almost AOR-style record. It is easy on the ear, tuneful, and not particularly demanding. It does 'feel' like a Yes album, but not the 1970s-style record that fans might have wanted and expected after such a remarkable tour. What we get is the sort of album they might have produced in place of *Big Generator*. Indeed, had the band made this album as a follow-up to *90125*, it might well have sold millions. As it was, it received poor reviews – unfairly, it has to be said – and failed to reach a mass audience distracted by the new 'punk', Grunge. The band did tour the album in North and South America and Japan, with Billy Sherwood providing backup guitar, but with audience numbers dropping, Rabin and Kaye both decided to move on. It was all change once again.

'The Calling' (Rabin, Anderson, Squire)
The mixture of acoustic and electric guitars in the initial riff, White's pounding 4 / 4 drum pattern, and the backing vocals – dominated by Rabin – set the tone for the whole album. In fact, this is an impressive opening track, with a lead vocal from Anderson and a catchy chorus. Indeed, catchy choruses are a feature of this album, tending to swamp the more progressive moments. There's a brief, impressive instrumental section halfway through the piece that shifts into far more Yes-like territory, although the solo section – with organ and country-style guitar swapping solos – is more conventional. The 2002 reissue includes a 'special' version of the song, which adds just over one minute via an ambient middle section which fails to add much to the piece.

'I Am Waiting' (Rabin, Anderson)
This is one of the most impressive pieces on the album, anchored by a beautiful guitar melody from Rabin, and a fragile, romantic vocal melody which sounds like it was written by Anderson. Again, White's drum sound is hardly subtle, but it's certainly great to hear Anderson so involved creatively. There's a hard rock 'break down' midway through the song – sung by Rabin – that jars slightly, but otherwise, this is an admirably restrained piece, and all the better for it.

'Real Love' (Squire, Rabin, Anderson)
Squire has always been excellent at writing brooding epics – see also 'The More We Live, Let go' – and here we get another very impressive piece, with plenty of menace in the opening verses, sung by Anderson, before Squire and Rabin blend voices as the song builds in power. This is one of the heaviest songs of the Rabin (or indeed any) Yes era – releasing into a pounding, heavy – but once again supremely catchy – chorus. Of all the songs on the album, 'Real Love' would have sat most easily on *Big Generator*. It is a big, heavy mini-masterpiece.

'State of Play' (Rabin, Anderson)
This may feel like a minor track after the heft of 'Real Love', but 'State Of Play' is a little gem, the equivalent on *Talk* of 'Our Song' from *90125*, opening

with a lovely acoustic guitar riff and the three vocalists blending nicely. It is the soaring chorus sung by Anderson that really impresses, however, as does Rabin's 'Elephant Talk'-style guitar. It's hardly an 'important' song in the catalogue, but as a piece of superbly-crafted pop-rock, it really stands out.

'Walls' (Rabin, Roger Hodgson, Anderson)
The same cannot be said, however, of this lightweight piece sung (mainly) by Rabin and co-written by Roger Hodgson of Supertramp fame. It has a decent chorus and instrumentally, it impresses at the halfway mark, with Squire's most notable bass contribution on an album where his playing is tediously conventional in the main. This was clearly intended as a single, and while it is decent enough, it was never going to be a hit.

'Where Will You Be' (Rabin, Anderson)
This is another interesting piece, hinting at another potential path for the band, should they have chosen to take it, towards 'World Music' (a phrase I've always found supremely patronising). But here, the song is built around a great melody from Anderson, while Rabin weaves some delightful Eastern textures around it and White delivers an insistent, repetitive percussion pattern. This is skilled stuff from both an arrangement and a production point of view. There's an extended solo from Rabin that doesn't outstay its welcome, and overall the piece is another quiet gem on an album full of them.

'Endless Dream' (Rabin, Anderson)
It is often felt that the lesser Yes albums – of which this is one – live or die by the quality of their epics, and 'Endless Dream' tends to get a lot of love as the 'redeeming' track on the album. However, for me, it is an unconvincing piece, good in parts but ultimately lengthy for the sake of it, without any of the twists and turns of (say) 'Awaken'. It begins well, with Rabin's heavy fusion instrumental 'Silent Spring', and the 'Talk' section, which again begins with a Rabin vocal, before a more extended section sung by Anderson which goes in a few interesting places. Had the track ended there, it might have made for an excellent closer, but after an ambient section and a reprise of the 'Silent Spring' piano riff, the song ratchets itself up another level with even more drama and the final 'so take your time' section to a slow fade ...

Your opinion may vary, of course, and there are many who love the emotion of this piece, but for me, 'Endless Dream' is – indeed – endless, a disappointing close to an otherwise excellent album.

The Keys to Ascension (1996) / The Keys to Ascension 2 (1997) / Keystudio (2001)

Personnel:
Jon Anderson: vocals, guitar, harp
Steve Howe: guitars, vocals
Chris Squire: bass, vocals
Alan White: drums, percussion, vocals
Rick Wakeman: keyboards
Studio tracks for The Keys To Ascension, produced by Yes and Tom Fletcher, mixed
by Billy Sherwood.
Recorded at Yesworld studio, San Luis Obispo, California. Recorded Autumn 1995 and Spring 1996
Released: October 1996
Highest chart places: UK: 48, USA: 99
Running time (studio tracks): 29:04
Studio tracks for The Keys To Ascension 2 produced by Yes and Billy Sherwood.
Recorded at 'The Office' , Van Nuys, California. Recorded: 1996
Released: November 1997
Highest chart places: UK: 62, USA: 159
Running time (studio tracks): 45:57

While Yes had suffered record company interference of some sort or other from the late 1970s onwards, the odd policy decisions that produced the strange *Keys to Ascension* project grew directly from new label Castle Communications. This British label wanted to release new Yes product – and I use the word 'product' advisedly – via their subsidiary Essential Records. The condition they placed on the idea was that they wanted the music to be produced by the 'classic' 1970s lineup that included Howe and Wakeman. The duo were asked to rejoin the band and duly accepted. Initially devised as a live project, it was agreed that the band should also record some new studio material, the whole project to be co-produced by American Tom Fletcher.

Anderson, Squire and White convened in Anderson's then-current home town, San Luis Obispo in California (North of Los Angeles, near the Pacific Coast) towards the end of 1995, with first Howe and then Wakeman joining the party shortly after. The band also rehearsed and played three live shows, filmed and recorded at the lovely Fremont Theatre in the same town in March 1996, while the initial studio tracks were recorded in the autumn of 1995 and the spring of 1996. Howe has referred to his own involvement in overseeing the mixing process of the live material (with some involvement from Anderson, who lived in San Luis Obispo) but with little interest from the rest of the band.

The resulting double album contains seven live tracks – including the first performance of 'The Revealing Science of God' since the *Tales* tour and also a rare live version of 'Onward' from *Tormato*, again unperformed up to that point. The band also include their ten-minute arrangement of 'America', which had rarely been played during the Wakeman era. However, the studio tracks have rather more of interest about them.

'Be the One (The One/ Humankind/ Skates)' (Anderson, Squire, Howe)

From the first notes of this first studio song, the problems are obvious. This is Anderson and Squire at their most aimless and turgid. Not that the piece is bad, as such, it's just somewhat lacklustre, sounding like a band rather tired of life rather than one that is recording together for the first time in seventeen years. Wakeman, in particular, sounds disengaged, as if his parts were added later without him contributing much to the arrangements, which they probably were, and he probably didn't. His synthesiser runs throughout the song are buried in the mix, so it is Howe that is left to contribute most of the lead work. The track shifts up a gear in the 'Humankind' section, but even this isn't particularly convincing.

'That, That Is (Togetherness / Crossfire / The Giving Things / That Is / All In All / How Did Heaven Begin / Agree To Agree)' (Anderson, Squire, Howe, White)

The album does pick up, however, with the nineteen-minute 'That, That Is'. More importantly, it starts well with a beautiful classical guitar piece from Howe, which, although it sounds like a solo track, holds the whole track together nicely, cropping up as an interlude here and there. Wakeman's keyboards compliment Howe's guitar well. The 'Crossfire' section – with a chanted introduction from Anderson – has both tension and energy, both factors missing from 'Be The One', while the brief 'The Giving Things' interlude is also rather lovely, based around an interesting guitar figure from Howe, whose sitar riff – shared with Wakeman – also dominates the 'That is' section. 'All in All' – with some head-turning piano from Wakeman – is also strong, and soars via its chorus. In fact, this is the section that feels like it should be the climax, but no, we have two more pieces, the pensive 'How Did Heaven Begin' and a return to the 'Crossfire' section, here called 'Agree to Agree', via a superb solo from Howe.

'That, This Is' is excellent in many ways; it has a high standard of material, even if it doesn't quite integrate it all effectively, feeling like a selection of bits rather than one fully realised piece of music. Wakeman is better integrated into the whole, however, so while it doesn't quite reach 'classic' status, it remains an enjoyable listen.

Although the album did not perform particularly well, reaching 46 in the UK and 99 in the US charts, a second instalment was ordered using the remaining live tracks – this time mixed by Billy Sherwood. Sherwood also agreed to record studio tracks, working with Wakeman for the first time. Compared to the comparatively tentative material on the first volume, the 45 minutes of material on volume two is much stronger and cohesive, even if it doesn't quite hang together as a complete album in its own right. However, In 'Mind Drive', the band produced their strongest piece of music of the 1990s.

'Mind Drive' (Anderson, Squire, White, Howe, Wakeman)
Like 'That, that Is', 'Mind Drive' begins with an excellent classical piece by Howe, with the theme then taken on impressively by Squire on bass. However, this already feels like more of a 'band' track, with the main staccato theme– propelled by Squire and White – and powerful orchestral-style keyboard work from Wakeman before the opening, powerful vocal salvo. This section was originally written by Squire and White for XYZ, and it sounds harder-edged as a result. Again, the band feel far more integrated here, with the track swinging through various sections – quiet and loud – while still sounding like they are playing the same piece of music. Eleven minutes in, the track leaps into another gear with fine organ and guitar solos and then a return to the dramatic main theme, which again gives solos to Howe and then Wakeman, delivering a brief synthesiser-organ solo followed by – gasp – his first proper Minimoog solo on a Yes studio album since *Tales*. It is a thrilling way to end an excellent piece of music.

Much liked by the band, sections of the piece were used as part of a medley of songs on the 2004 world tour in a section that also included 'South Side of the Sky' and 'Turn of the Century'. It remains the most impressive piece of music from the *Keys to Ascension* era.

'Foot Prints' (Anderson, Squire, Howe, White)
While 'Foot Prints' does not quite maintain the energy of 'Mind Drive' it does benefit from a strong, almost Beatle-esque melody, and while Wakeman gets no writing credit, his parts are crucial – including more Minimoog (really, Mr Wakeman, you spoil us!) and his parts are well placed in the mix. In the meantime, Howe's contributions feel less like solo tracks shoehorned in and seem better integrated into the whole. 'Foot Prints' continues the high standard set by 'Mind Drive'. The brief 'My Eyes' *a capella* section, was also played within the 'Mind Drive' melody on tour in 2004.

'Bring Me To The Power' (Anderson, Howe)
Starting superbly with some fine drumming from White, 'Bring Me To The Power' doesn't quite maintain the standard set by the opening two tracks, despite some fine ensemble playing from the band, particularly Howe, in jazz guitar mode. Frustratingly, the most interesting playing is just hinted at, with Squire's bass prominent, in the low-volume section just over a minute from the end. Overall, this piece seems underdeveloped and a little rushed in its execution.

'Children of Light (Children of Light)' (Anderson, Vangelis, Squire) / 'Lifeline' (Wakeman, Howe)

The Keystudio version features an introduction called 'Lightening' written by Rick Wakeman, but shortens the main part of the track by a verse.

Originally envisioned as a Jon and Vangelis piece – thus, the writing credit for the famous Greek musician – 'Children of Light' doesn't quite feel like a Yes track. However, it is certainly a decent piece of material. The coda, 'Lifeline', feels tacked on, although it might have worked as a short track in its own right or as an introduction to another piece. The introductory synthesiser instrumental, 'Lightening', is perfectly fine, although again, it seems out of place.

'Sign Language' (Wakeman, Howe)

This is a second example of Howe and Wakeman writing an instrumental track together, a very rare occurrence. As a piece, it is rather lovely, Howe soloing over orchestral keyboards from Wakeman. It really has no place on a Yes album, though, on its own. It sounds like it was written as a section of a longer track but not developed further.

All the studio tracks were gathered together as one – cheaply produced – compilation *KeyStudio* in 2001. This version adds the Wakeman-penned introduction to 'Children of Light', which was originally vetoed by the rest of the band. Even placed in a different order, the songs feel like individual tracks rather than a cohesive album. In fact, if you look over all the studio tracks recorded during 1995 and 1996 for the *Keys to Ascension* project, they must go down as an opportunity wasted. Although 'That, That Is' is, in itself, a decent piece of work (even if it feels like a few disparate pieces thrown together), a lot of the material recorded later – with more creative input from Wakeman – and appearing on *Keys 2* is a lot better. However, only 'Mind Drive' and 'Footprints' feel like fully rounded, finished pieces. To work as an album on its own – and the band might have done just that – *Keystudio* really needs another long track. However, the pieces on the two albums are still worth hearing, if only for 'Mind Drive'.

When the band completed the final studio tracks towards the end of 1996, the label sat on them for many months – releasing *Keys to Ascension 2* in November 1997 just before the next Yes album, *Open Your Eyes* was about to hit the streets, to some confusion.

YES ... On Track

Open Your Eyes (1997)

Personnel:
Jon Anderson: lead vocals
Steve Howe: guitars, steel guitar, mandolin, banjo, vocals
Billy Sherwood: guitars, vocals, keyboards
Chris Squire: bass guitar, vocals, harmonica
Alan White: drums, percussion, vocals
Igor Khoroshev: keyboards on 'Fortune Seller', 'No Way We Can Lose', and 'New State of Mind'
Steve Porcaro: keyboards on 'Open Your Eyes'
Produced by Yes. Recording and mixing by Billy Sherwood 'The Office' , Van Nuys, California.
Released: November 1997
Highest chart positions: UK: Did not chart. USA: 151.
Running time: 74:12 (including 'The Source')

As mentioned before, Yes albums have been created in different ways over the years. We have already seen that the *Keys To Ascension* project originated from a specific financial deal. But rarely in as convoluted a way as their second offering of late 1997, *Open Your Eyes*. The album had several catalysts. Firstly, another rift with Rick Wakeman over touring schedules meant that they were without a keyboard player. Secondly, the band's new management – Left Bank – having put together a plan for the band, suggested – in a moment of misguided hope – that they develop material that Squire had been working on for an album with Billy Sherwood in California, called Conspiracy. Several part-recorded tracks were offered up by the pair, and then worked on remotely by the rest of the band. Despite the writing credits being democratically split between Anderson, Squire, White, Sherwood and Howe, it is clear that a huge amount of the writing was done by Sherwood and Squire, with White, Howe and Anderson having relatively little creative input except on the piece 'From A Balcony'. Howe has claimed that even though Left Bank management and Billy Sherwood felt that Anderson's vocals and Howe's playing would give the material that 'Yes character' it needed, he disagreed vociferously, feeling that fans would be alienated by the style of the material that Squire and Sherwood were producing, which, after all, had never been intended for Yes. He did, however, agree to the permanent recruitment of Sherwood as long as Igor Khoroshev was recruited on keyboards for the subsequent tour. The Russian was an acquaintance of Anderson and a highly talented musician, with a flamboyant style somewhere between Moraz and Wakeman. He came in at the end of the recording to play on a few songs, although his true musical character was not to appear until *The Ladder*.

Released in November 1997, just a few weeks after *Keys to Ascension 2,* the album sank without trace, confusing casual fans and in the main irritating die-hard ones. Howe was correct. In the continual internet chatter amongst fans about 'which Yes album is the worst', it often wins. However, as a rock album in its own right, it stands up pretty well. It is certainly as good as the final version of *Conspiracy* by Squire and Sherwood, which gets a much more favourable press amongst those that have heard it. It is one of the best albums that Sherwood has been involved in, and he has every right to be proud of his work. However, to take a dominant composer, impose him on an established rock band and expect it to work is ambitious in the extreme. Although it worked with Trevor Rabin in 1983, that was a very particular set of circumstances, and Rabin was – and remains – a musician of the highest calibre. On *Open Your Eyes*, Anderson does seem a little superimposed on the music, with Sherwood's own vocals often almost as dominant. Furthermore, decent though most of the songs are, the album does feel a little homogenous after a while – something rarely levelled at this most eclectic of bands. There are a lot of good things on the album, but it all seems overproduced and under-composed somehow. In short, while *Open Your Eyes* is a decent rock album, it is not a good Yes album.

However, it did lead to a new lease of life for the band as a touring outfit, as a six-piece, and the *Open Your Eyes* tour was an artistic and commercial success, with Khoroshev, in particular, fitting into the band exceptionally well.

'New State Of Mind' (Anderson, Howe, Sherwood, Squire, White)
This opening track has a rather bold swagger to it and some good pedal steel and lead work from Howe. However, the vocals act as a template for what is to come – they are massed and overproduced, with Anderson barely audible at times. It's a strong enough start, but at six minutes, it probably overstays its welcome by around two of those.

'Open Your Eyes' (Anderson, Howe, Sherwood, Squire, White)
The title track is probably the strongest piece on the album, particularly as it feels a little apart from many of the other songs. It's a good piece of pop/rock with a strong, catchy chorus and with Anderson prominent, but also some great vocals from Squire, who actually shares lead vocal duties briefly in the verses. It deserved its place in the live set for the subsequent tour, has a nice sense of dynamics and it also gives Howe an opportunity to rip through a fine, if brief, solo.

'Universal Garden' (Anderson, Howe, Sherwood, Squire, White)
Another strong song, this begins very promisingly with a lovely classical guitar intro from Howe and a pleasingly off-kilter verse sung by Anderson. It becomes rather more conventional in the chorus, however, yet there's still some room for dynamics, with more acoustic textures from Howe, even if Sherwood's orchestral keyboards are a little ham-fisted. In fact, the band might have developed this track further – it has the aura of a ten-minute piece squeezed into a somewhat compressed six minutes. Nonetheless, it's

rather decent and somewhat unsung. Howe, again, makes the best of limited opportunities.

'No Way We Can Lose' (Anderson, Howe, Sherwood, Squire, White)
At this point, the album goes off the rails somewhat. This song – a simple plea for cooperation in life – has Sherwood's solo work written all over it, and – at best – has the tone of a Trevor Rabin pop song, but without the inspiration that Rabin might have brought to it. Squire plays harmonica at one point, and the whole thing is just too twee to work as a Yes piece, tuneful though it is.

'Fortune Seller' (Anderson, Howe, Sherwood, Squire, White)
Another of the stronger tracks, this once again has some decent playing, including a fine synthesiser solo from Khoroshev that is almost buried in the mix, while his organ solo later in the song is somewhat more prominent. Again, the piece probably tries to go in too many places crammed into five minutes and really ought to have taken its time to develop. The overall impression is that of a bit of a mess, but the song has to be applauded for its ambition.

'Man In The Moon' (Anderson, Howe, Sherwood, Squire, White)
Ah, the track that had Yes fans reaching for the 'skip' button in their thousands. Anderson and Sherwood sing a trite melody in unison against a simple guitar and keyboard riff. Even I, who have no patience with the 'It's not Yes unless it's ten minutes long' camp, can see that this is a mistake – not as a song, necessarily, but as a song on a Yes album. The sing-song chorus may tempt the listener to contemplate violence.

'Wonderlove' (Anderson, Howe, Sherwood, Squire, White)
'Wonderlove' has another strong start, sounding like an Anderson / Howe collaboration. However, the song itself is probably the weakest on the record. Howe saves proceedings with his best solo of the album, but otherwise, this is forgettable stuff and should probably have been abandoned at the demo stage.

'From A Balcony' (Anderson, Howe, Sherwood, Squire, White)
Whereas the sing-song melody of 'Man In The Moon' was just too cloying, here a sweet melody works rather better. This short piece – also played on the subsequent tour – is a collaboration between Anderson and Howe. It's not their finest work – it feels underdeveloped, almost an afterthought, but it's a welcome relief from the dense and somewhat overproduced Sherwood tracks.

'Love Shine' (Anderson, Howe, Sherwood, Squire, White)
This is one of those Sherwood pieces, but a very strong one, it has to be said. It is another exuberant pop/rock song with a winning chorus (bolstered by a

lively lead run/riff from Howe). Sherwood's keyboards also move away from the orchestral stabs ubiquitous on the rest of the album, and Squire's backing vocals are excellent. The chorus is a real ear-worm too, and while it's not very Yes, it is genuinely over too soon. A little gem.

'Somehow...Someday' (Anderson, Howe, Sherwood, Squire, White)
Anderson kicks this one off with one of his favourite Celtic melodies, also used in the song 'O'er' on his solo album *The Promise Ring*, before the main song – a stately but faintly dull plod – kicks in. Again, it's not bad but just a bit forgettable, and that re-used melody seems a bit pointless.

'The Solution' (Anderson, Howe, Sherwood, Squire, White)
The final track has a nice sense of drama and is the only song on the album to really 'rock out', but even then, it's all a bit stop-start, with three good hooks 'the solution..', 'down we go' and 'giving in, giving out'. Unable to choose between them, it gives us all three rather randomly. This is a problem of arrangement rather than composition, but it is frustrating, meaning that the album ends on a whimper rather than a bang. A shame.

'The Source' (Anderson, Howe, Sherwood, Squire, White)
A long ambient track – mainly simulated bird noise (see 'Close To The Edge') and waves crashing on a shore, but also featuring snatches from the album. The piece appears as a 'hidden' track at the end of 'The Solution'.

Related tracks
'Wish I Knew'. (Squire, Sherwood)
Source: Chris Squire and Billy Sherwood, Conspiracy
A rudimentary, early version of 'Open Your Eyes' sung by Squire which leaves the chorus until far later in the song, and misses Anderson and Howe badly.

'Man In The Moon'. (Squire, Sherwood)
Source: Chris Squire and Billy Sherwood, Conspiracy.
Pretty much the same song and arrangement, but with no Anderson.

The Ladder (1999)

Jon Anderson: lead vocals
Steve Howe: lead and acoustic guitars, steel guitar, mandolin, backing vocals
Billy Sherwood: guitars, backing vocals
Chris Squire: bass guitars, backing vocals
Alan White: drums, percussion, backing vocals
Igor Khoroshev: keyboards, backing vocals
Randy Raine-Reusch: world instruments
Rhys Fulber: dance loops
The Marguerita Horns: horns on 'Lightning Strikes'
Tom Keenlyside: piccolo, tenor saxophone
Derry Burns: trumpet
Rod Murray: trombone
Tom Colclough: alto saxophone
Neil Nicholson: tuba
Produced by Bruce Fairbairn at Armoury Sudios, Kitsilano, Vancouver, Canada.
Engineering and mixing: Mike Plotnikoff
Recorded: February to May 1999
Released: September 1999
Highest chart places: UK: 36, USA: 99
Running time: 60:19

As the turbulent 90s came to an end, Yes found themselves with something close to a stable line up. With Anderson, Howe, Squire and White providing a core that would last almost ten years, the band kept faith with the musicians that had toured with *Open Your Eyes*, with Igor Khoroschev and Billy Sherwood becoming full members.

Via the band's management, they were introduced to famed Canadian record producer Bruce Fairbairn. Fairbairn had a very impressive track record, having produced – amongst many others – huge hit albums for Bon Jovi, Aerosmith and AC/DC. While he had no direct experience with progressive rock bands, it was felt an experienced producer would help lend a new ear and a new structure to the band's material. The group upped sticks and recorded at Armoury Studios in Vancouver, although Fairbairn was, tragically, to die during the mixing of the album in May 1999.

However, the producer's track record and positive attitude meant that he won instant respect from even the most seasoned and egotistical members of the band, helping mould the material into something that genuinely feels cohesive and well-constructed. *The Ladder* does contain some good writing, mixing song-orientated material with two longer pieces – 'Homeworld' and 'New Language'. Indeed, taken track by track, the album is fine. And yet, as a complete package, it fails to satisfy. Given that the band had the capacity – with Sherwood's songwriting and production ability and Khoroshev's obvious virtuosity – they might have been more adventurous. Even though the band plays well and sounds fully committed, there's a lack of depth throughout.

However, complexty was not Fairbairn's style, and the result is lacklustre, not really the sort of album any Yes fans might have wanted. As a result, it languishes in a sort of netherworld, neither hated like *Open Your Eyes* or *Heaven and Earth* but not loved either. Nor does it elicit the amount of debate that some of the more controversial albums receive. While loved by some, for many people – including this author – it languishes in mediocrity.

These last few years of the Twentieth Century were the commercial nadir for Yes, and while it did better than *Open Your Eyes*, The Ladder reached 36 in the UK for one week only and a poor 99 in the USA. Once again, an attempt at a more 'commercial' direction had failed them badly. The band did play a good portion of this long album live – the last time their set contained such a high proportion of songs from the 'current' album.

'Homeworld (The Ladder)' (Anderson, Howe, Squire, White, Khoroshev, Sherwood)

By far the most impressive track on the album, the nine-minute 'Homeworld' is the only piece that can be considered 'progressive rock' from start to finish. Opening with an interesting, almost bluegrass-style guitar figure, the song develops into a powerful, mid-tempo tour de force, with a keyboard-orientated mid-section that recalls some of the band's finest pieces. Anderson sings with controlled passion, and while the backing vocals are somewhat over-produced, there is some fine instrumental work from Khoroshev and Howe, in particular. The pensive, acoustic close to the track is also beautiful, with some lovely piano from the Russian. Played live on *The Ladder* Tour only, a live version also appears on the 'tour' version of the album, which has an extra CD.

'It Will Be A Good Day (The River)' (Anderson, Howe, Squire, White, Khoroshev, Sherwood)

And then the mediocrity sets in. 'It Will Be A Good Day' is perfectly decent. It has a pleasing melody and an upbeat, positive lyric from Anderson. The music has a strong feeling of Howe about it and the backing vocals, with Sherwood prominent, are nicely done, acting as a counterpoint to the main vocal. It all works nicely, but settles into something of a mid-paced dirge with little in the arrangement to make it distinctive. It was played live on *The Ladder* Tour only.

'Lightning Strikes' (Anderson, Howe, Squire, White, Khoroshev, Sherwood)

This lively, throwaway piece – released as a single in 1999 – introduces a strong African influence, with some great acoustic guitar from Howe, and – gasp – the first horn arrangement on a Yes record since the *Big Generator* album. The track actually goes off in some quite interesting directions, but it's too short and lightweight to make a great impact. It is good fun, though. Again, it was played live on *The Ladder* Tour only.

'Can I?' (Anderson, Howe, Squire, White, Khoroshev, Sherwood)
This short piece reprises 'We Have Heaven' from *Fragile* with a strong Australian aboriginal arrangement. It's a nice idea and acts as a fun introduction to ...

'Face to Face' (Anderson, Howe, Squire, White, Khoroshev, Sherwood)
The African influences on 'Lightning Strikes' continue for this upbeat song, led by Squire's joyful bass riff and some unusual keyboard effects. In fact, of the shorter songs, this is my favourite – it has a genuinely exuberant quality and some beautifully-arranged backing vocals. It also has a key change towards the end that comes as a pleasant – rather than jarring – surprise. With a little judicious editing, this might have made a far better – and more Yes-like – single than the more 'obvious' 'Lightening Strikes'. A standout, beautifully arranged track. It was played live on *The Ladder* Tour only.

'If Only You Knew' (Anderson, Howe, Squire, White, Khoroshev, Sherwood)
Unfortunately, the shift in quality cannot be maintained. 'If Only You Knew' is a competent, mid-tempo ballad. Again, it has a fair amount going for it melodically, and the arrangement is fine, but there's nothing about it that makes the listener want to listen to it multiple times.

'To Be Alive (Hep Yadda)' (Anderson, Howe, Squire, White, Khoroshev, Sherwood)
Again, 'World' influences are to the fore – this time an Asian influence – on another melodic, rather mediocre pop song. Anderson's positive outlook on life is again emphasised in the lyrics, and Howe throws in a splendid pedal steel solo. Anderson is the star of this piece, but overall it is the pop side of the band that is to the fore, making this somewhat forgettable.

'Finally' (Anderson, Howe, Squire, White, Khoroshev, Sherwood)
Yes rock out a little with Anderson turning on his 'rock' voice. This is powerful stuff, very much in the style that Fairbairn was used to producing. Yes rock out pretty well, and the track is nicely done, probably the most 'produced' song on the album. The guitar solo in the first half sounds like it is played by Sherwood. The song takes an interesting twist just over halfway in, with an ambient, unconvincing, supposedly-emotive close based around a decent Howe solo.

'The Messenger' (Anderson, Howe, Squire, White, Khoroshev, Sherwood)
Yes have a go at reggae. Prompted to write about one of his heroes by Fairbairn, Anderson wrote a song about Bob Marley. In fact, the 'reggae' part

is more of an influence than anything, informing the arrangement without dominating it. The song expands into an inventive rock song with a decent chorus and a nice coda. One of the stronger pieces on the record, this might have been expanded with the coda acting as a bridge for another section and then a return to the chorus, meaning that to me, it feels unfinished. Played live on *The Ladder* Tour only, a live version also appears on the 'tour' version of the album.

'New Language' (Anderson, Howe, Squire, White, Khoroshev, Sherwood)
'New Language' has a terrific opening – an opportunity for Khoroshev to rock out on church organ, then Hammond organ, backed by a full-steam band arrangement. Two minutes in, however, we return to normal service with a jaunty, poppy song with Anderson's solo work written all over it. It does return briefly to something approaching progressive rock, but then the jaunty pop song returns to taunt us. Howe does give us a really good instrumental section with an acoustic guitar solo with full rock backing, and an unusual instrumental touch, showing some invention in the arrangement. There's a really good epic piece in here, but the structure isn't quite right, despite a powerful ending.

'Nine Voices (Longwalker)' (Anderson, Howe, Squire, White, Khoroshev, Sherwood)
'Nine Voices', which Anderson wrote about the 'Longest walk' in 1978 – a spiritual walk across the USA by native Americans in protest against anti-Native American legislation, closes the album strongly. It is essentially a piece for Portuguese guitar and voice, and ends the album in fine, melodic style.

Its simplicity has allowed the song a decent life beyond *The Ladder* tour, occasionally played at live shows as recently as 2018. Ironically, it wasn't played on *The Ladder* Tour itself.

Magnification (2001)

Personnel:
Jon Anderson: vocals, midi guitar, acoustic guitar
Steve Howe: acoustic and electric guitars, pedal steel, mandolin, vocals
Chris Squire: bass and vocals
Alan White: drums, percussion, vocals and piano
Produced by Yes and Tim Weidner
Executive Producer Jordan Berliant Engineered by Tim Weidner
Recorded at Sound Design Studios, Santa Barbara
Orchestral Music composed, arranged and conducted by Larry Groupé Recorded:
Spring and Summer 2001
Released: September 2001
Highest chart places: UK: 71, USA: 186

With Igor Khoroshev now installed on keyboards but Billy Sherwood having decided to move on, the band undertook their *Masterworks* tour of the USA in 2000, playing long-form pieces (like 'The Gates of Delirium') which allowed them to make excellent use of the Russian's versatility and virtuosity. However, his behaviour on tour became a problem, and at the end of it, he was fired.

This left the band with no keyboard player, so – ever one to see an opportunity when it presents itself – Anderson suggested they return to the format of *Time And A Word* and record with an orchestra. Long-time Yes fan Larry Groupé was employed to compose and conduct the orchestra, and the band settled down to write in California, with Howe joining them later from his home in the UK.

With Producer Tim Weidner at the helm, the band soon swapped from analogue recording to digital, using Pro Tools, as it became very clear early on that the complexities of melding band and orchestra together were best achieved using the flexibility that digital recording provides. Steve Howe has reported that the album was difficult to complete, with the placing of his own guitars within the context of the orchestral arrangements a particular challenge, and that, as with the live recordings on the *Keys To Ascension* albums, he was somewhat left 'holding the baby'. Additionally, the roles of Weidner and Jordan Berliant – then of Left Bank Management – were also crucial to the completion of the album.

Despite its commercial failure, *Magnification* is a strong latter-day Yes album, and the orchestra is nicely integrated with the band. Indeed some of Groupé's orchestral pieces – when the band is not playing – are strong enough to make me want to hear more of his work away from the band. The lack of a keyboard player also allows Howe to sweep in and out of the mix with the full range of his guitar palette, despite his own unhappiness at how much he was restricted. From reading this book up to this point, you will know that I am a big fan of keyboards as part of the Yes sound, and yet

– knowing that this was a one-off project – I don't miss the swirling organs or the screaming Moogs at all here. Yet this was to be the band's last studio album for ten years.

Magnification was to become the focus of the band's touring for the next two years, firstly via the Symphonic tour, which saw the band play small arenas with an orchestra, with talented US keyboard player Tom Brislin guesting – and the 2003 tour, which saw yet another return from Rick Wakeman – but still saw 'Magnification' and 'In the Presence of...' in the set.

'Magnification' (Anderson, Howe, Squire, White)
Considering how important the orchestra was to be on the album, it would have been perfectly reasonable to expect some sort of overture, yet it is Steve Howe's guitar that begins this fine opening song, and he dominates throughout, with the orchestra providing support. This does – genuinely – feel like Yes, with some moments of complexity and some prominent bass and backing vocals from Squire, albeit within the framework of a 'song' which has a very decent hook. This song was played on both the 2002 Symphonic Tour and in 2003 with Wakeman on keyboards.

'Spirit of Survival' (Anderson, Howe, Squire, White)
The opening track segues atmospherically into this, the 'heaviest' song on the album, although it's unusually rendered, via bass, drums and stabs (almost like 'Owner Of A Lonely Heart') of orchestra, leaving Howe to solo. Squire delivers another great riff here, with hints of Duane Eddy's 'Peter Gunn'. Again, it's an impressive piece that might have been a great live track.

'Don't Go' (Anderson, Howe, Squire, White)
Deliberately catchy and clearly intended as a possible hit single (it wasn't), this quirky song with simple love-gone-awry lyrics has a catchy guitar riff and one of those unexpectedly-complex-yet-simple-sounding choruses that gets into your head and won't leave. It's undemanding but rather charming and fun, even if Howe does overplay a little. The orchestra only comes into its own in the final seconds, reprising Howe's guitar figure from earlier in the song, a nice piece of detail.

'Give Love Each Day' (Anderson, Howe, Squire, White)
This song begins with an extended orchestral passage, and it's utterly glorious. It was used as part of the orchestral overture to the Symphonic Tour. The song itself is fine – with Anderson linking his two favourite subjects – eternal, redeeming love and native cultures – into an unashamedly romantic song with the orchestra sweeping in and out of the mix. It's a lovely song, but the orchestral opening is better!

'Can You Imagine?' (Anderson, Howe, Squire, White)
At less than three minutes, this is a brief but memorable song featuring a great orchestral arrangement, some rare piano from White, chiming guitar from Howe and an equally rare lead vocal from Squire, with Anderson providing all the backing vocals. It originally began life as a piece developed by XYZ – Squire and White's short-lived band with Jimmy Page of Led Zeppelin – but here it works beautifully as a Yes track, albeit a short one.

'We Agree' (Anderson, Howe, Squire, White)
Despite some very classy classical guitar from Howe, and a decent chorus, this mediocre song is the least impressive piece on the album, feeling rather like an outtake from an Anderson solo album. Given that *Magnification* is over 60 minutes long, it might perhaps have helped the playability of the album had it been dropped, although it's by no means unlistenable, and the orchestral arrangement certainly has its moments.

'Soft As A Dove' (Anderson, Howe, Squire, White)
The same might apply to this brief piece, which does showcase Howe's classical guitar and some solo flute, but feels rather pointless and sentimental thanks to Anderson's underdeveloped, rather aimless vocal melody.

'Dreamtime' (Anderson, Howe, Squire, White)
Howe's acoustic playing is outstanding on this album, and his duet with the solo violin on the opening of this piece is delightful, as is the use of the orchestra, with the brass section particularly impressive. Anderson sings the verse with accompaniment from the orchestra only, before the arrival of the whole band, and again this is powerful stuff, with White's drumming very impressive, and Squire's prominent bass seemingly effortless. This is the piece on the album that best integrates the band and the orchestra and, given the relative amount of attention paid to 'In The Presence Of ', feels – at just under eleven minutes – like a lost classic. If you haven't heard *Magnification,* this – and the following piece – are worth the price of admission alone. The track also finishes with another two-minute orchestral piece, this time with hints of Leonard Bernstein.

'In The Presence Of (Deeper / Death Of Ego / True Believer / Turn Around And Remember)' (Anderson, Howe, Squire, White)
This closing epic was played on most of the live shows over two tours in 2002-2003 and it's not hard to understand why. It's a beautiful, romantic piece in four parts that packs a real emotional punch via Anderson's heart-wrenching vocal melody on the 'Deeper' section, and also features White's piano once again. The 'Death Of Ego' features some further wordy musings from Anderson, with the orchestra providing the main support with some fine soloing from Howe before 'True Believer' returns to the main melody.

The final section 'Turn Around And Remember' – heralded by a climbing bass figure from Squire and Howe's pedal steel – builds in intensity slowly, again with band and orchestra in harmony. This is marvellous music, pure and simple, exquisitely progressive without the frenetic attack of the younger band.

'Time Is Time' (Anderson, Howe, Squire, White)
A lightweight, somewhat unnecessary coda after the heft of the previous track, featuring some lovely solo violin but little else. It did make it into the acoustic set on the 2004 world tour, but was rather overshadowed by classier material.

Related tracks
None, although various versions were released with a second CD, which contained various live versions from the *Symphonic* tour. I have the UK tour version, which includes live versions of 'Magnification', 'In the Presence Of' and 'The Gates of Delirium' plus low-resolution videos of 'Don't Go', 'The Gates Of Delirium' and a short video interview with Jon Anderson.

Fly From Here (2011) / Fly from Here – Return Trip (2018)

Personnel:
Benoît David: vocals (2011 version only)
Chris Squire: bass, vocals
Steve Howe: electric and acoustic guitars, vocals
Alan White: drums
Geoff Downes: keyboards, vocals
Oliver Wakeman: keyboards
Luis Jardin: percussion
Trevor Horn: additional vocals and keyboards, lead vocals (Return trip)
Gerard Johnson: piano
Produced by Trevor Horn at: Sarm West, London: Sarm West Coast, Los Angeles: Langley Studios, Devon: Schwarz Studios, Sussex
Engineered and mixed by Tim Weidner
Recorded: October 2010 to February 2011, Return Trip version 2016-2017.
Released: June 2011
Highest chart places: UK: 30, USA: 36
Running time: 2011 version: 47:28, Return Trip: 53:37

Even though it had been almost ten years since the band's last studio album, life – as usual – had not run smoothly for Yes. The first years of the new millennium saw a period of intense touring. The band played with full orchestra for the Symphonic Tour in 2002, while a return to the band of Rick Wakeman saw them celebrate 35 years in 2003, followed by a longer world tour in 2004 playing larger venues. This period is extensively documented on DVD. By the end of the Summer of 2004, the band – exhausted – went on hiatus. A 40th-anniversary tour was planned, but with Wakeman unwilling to take on such extensive touring – at least at the time – his son Oliver, whose style is more florid than his keyboardist brother Adam, was drafted in to 'keep it in the family'. A serious respiratory illness to Jon Anderson, however, delayed plans and the band eventually took the decision to tour without him. Anderson would not be associated directly with the name Yes for almost ten years.

Drafting in French Canadian singer Benoît David from Yes tribute band Close To The Edge, the band toured for the next two years, playing essentially 'greatest hit' sets but also drafting in material from Drama.

So to *Fly From Here*. The lineup – including Oliver Wakeman and Benoît David – began work in 2010 on new material, the plan initially being for Howe and Wakeman to produce the album. Many of the tracks that were included in the second half of the final recording were worked up during this period, and the band went into Trevor Horns' studio SARM West in Los Angeles at the end of 2010 to begin recording with Horn himself – at least partially – involved.

The band decided to use the song 'We Can Fly From Here' that Horn and Downes had offered as their 'entre' to the band back in 1980, and further plans were made to use other Horn / Downes songs from the same period, which culminated in the decision to build these compositions into a 24-minute suite. However, Wakeman was replaced by Geoff Downes at the end of 2010, taking his own songs with him, and the rest of the sessions in the early part of 2011 took place with Downes on keyboards, Horn in an overseeing role and Tim Weidner again engineering and mixing.

This had been a traumatic ten years for Yes, with first Jon Anderson being – it would certainly seem – ousted (according to many of the wider Yes community) and the same happening to another Yes family member in Oliver so, with the band now signed to Italian rock label Frontiers, there was a great deal of interest in how the album would sound. And the result? While it is a long way from the orchestral grandiosity of *Magnification*, to me this is the best Yes album since *Talk* and while some of the methods to get to it may have been dubious, the end it made for a convincing record. The Horn / Downes material is very strong in its own way, with quality melodies and songwriting at the fore and while the other material doesn't quite match it, the album hangs together very well. The 'gimmick' of, to all intents and purposes, 'buying in' high-quality material from another, albeit highly credible, source turned out to be inspired. Would the album that the Wakeman lineup was working on have been better? This is yet another Yes 'what if '...

And yet there was a further sting in the tale. In 2017, Following the death of Chris Squire in June 2015 and with Benoît David long since replaced, Trevor Horn himself, helped by Steve Howe and Geoff Downes and urged by Alan White, began a revised version of the album. The new version was released in March 2018 and included new lead vocals by Horn himself and David removed, plus some newly recorded parts by Howe and Downes. The album was also remixed, 'Hour of Need' extended and another song from 2011 'Don't Take No For An Answer' added.

There is a certain authenticity to having Horn sing the lead vocals, and yet I actually prefer David's singing, and the new mixes and parts, while nicely done, don't add a huge amount to the end result. It is hard, therefore, to feel strongly about the new version one way or the other. I like the original, and the new version is a nice addition to the catalogue, but is it essential and does it add a whole new dimension to the songs? Probably not. What Horn did do, however, was accentuate Squire's vocal and bass contributions, providing space in the arrangements where needed. At times, aside from his lead vocals, *The Return Trip* feels like a love letter to Horn's departed comrade. It's actually rather touching, in a way.

If I were to produce a 'perfect' version of this record, I'd leave Benoit on and 'Our of Need' untouched. I'd also leave off the Howe-penned solo track off, BUT use the *Return Trip* arrangements. But the chance of a *Return Return Trip* are almost zero.

'Fly From Here – overture' (Horn, Downes)
An 'Overture' in the correct sense of the word, this version introduces the music that is to come later on in the suite. There are differences between the two versions, but only subtle changes to the mix. The basic instrumentation remains the same.

'Fly From Here Part I – We Can Fly' (Horn, Downes, Squire)
This is the song that 'introduced' Horn and Downes to White, Squire and Howe in 1980, here on album in its full arrangement for the first time, although a live version from 1980 appears on the *The Word Is Live* live boxed set. It is very hard to deny the quality of the song itself, which is phenomenally catchy, to the extent that one wonders why it didn't appear on *Drama*. Squire's excellent harmony vocal blends very well with both Benoît David and Trevor Horn, depending on which version you prefer. *The Return Trip* version adds some new guitar and a revised ending, but otherwise tightens up the arrangement considerably, losing almost a minute from the original version. My preferred version doesn't exist, which would be Benoît's excellent lead vocal on the original version, but with the tightened arrangement of *The Return Trip*. Completists should note that a demo of the song appears on the expanded version of the second Buggles album *Adventures in Modern Recording*.

'Fly From Here Part II – Sad Night at the Airfield' (Horn, Downes)
This is another beautiful song from the sessions for the second Buggles album – a version of which made it onto the deluxe edition of *Adventures in Modern Recording*. It is also the track that had the largest reworking for the *Return Trip* version, with Horn taking a minute and a quarter off the 2011 original.

In the process, he added more classical guitar, and boosted Squire's backing vocal towards the end, giving it a somewhat poignant 'duet' feel. Again, the reworking works well, though the original definitely has more warmth, mainly provided by Benoît David's lush lead vocal. However, the song stays intact in either version, and it's charming.

'Fly From Here Part III – Madman at the Screens' (Horn, Downes)
Essentially expanding on the material in the 'Overture', this tense section moves the overall piece further into the realm of progressive rock – both versions even have an organ solo by Downes. It's a decent piece of music, and although, once again, the more recent version squeezes the arrangement a little, there's little to choose between them, although Horn once again gives Squire's backing vocals more prominence in the remixed 2018 version.

'Fly From Here Part IV – Bumpy Ride' (Howe)
Howe's quirky, largely instrumental 'Bumpy Ride', at just over two minutes long, survives completely intact in the 2018 version, aside from replacing the

Benoît David vocals with Trevor Horn. It's good fun – the sort of piece that the 'old' Yes would have used in the middle of a longer track – although some fans have taken against its quirkiness for some reason.

'Fly From Here Part V – We Can Fly (reprise)' (Horn, Downes, Squire)
We return to 'Fly From Here' for the conclusion, with few differences between the two versions, except for a longer fade-out in the *Return Trip* mix.

So, what should we make of the 'Fly From Here' suite? The band played it live on the tour, which followed the release of the album later in 2011 and it worked very well as a cohesive, nicely structured piece of music. It should be pointed out that for a 25-minute piece (22 in the 2018 version), it does include a lot of repeated material and relies on the strength of two admittedly excellent songs that had been written over 30 years previously. Yet as a piece of music in its own right, it does work incredibly well. To me, it is Yes' most impressive epic since *Drama*, and they have Horn and Downes to thank for it.

'The Man You Always Wanted Me To Be' (Squire, Johnson, Sessler)
The strength of the opening epic is in stark contrast to this somewhat lacklustre song from Squire, who also provides the lead vocal. In truth, it's not bad – certainly compared with some of the material on *Heaven and Earth* – but it's just a little mediocre, overstaying its welcome by a couple of minutes. Disappointing on first listen, it has grown on me somewhat over the years, but after the high standard set by the 'Fly From Here' suite, it still disappoints.

'Life On a Film Set' (Horn, Downes)
It's back to excellent material from Horn and Downes (again from 1980), albeit with a bit more of a progressive feel. A pensive opening verse gives way to an exuberant last four minutes, largely the same in both versions, with some excellent soloing from Howe. The 2018 version again boosts Squire's backing vocals. The Yes version is actually very similar to the Buggles version, again to be found on the deluxe version of *Adventures in Modern Recording*. It was played live in late 2011.

'Hour of Need' (Howe)
'Hour of Need', written by Howe, gives us a powerful glimpse of what the album with Oliver Wakeman might have sounded like. In its 2011 version, it's a slight but charming acoustic ditty, with a brief but characteristic, synthesiser solo from Oliver. To my ears, the song actually sounds like it was written for Jon Anderson. The longer 2018 version encases this song with a full-band intro and outro, essentially a showcase for Howe's lead guitar work. The two sections do not sound like they belong on the same track and the decision to drop these parts when the album was first released was probably the correct

one. The 2018 version has Horn in there, but with the lower-register vocals – probably by Howe as much as Squire – emphasised.

'Solitaire' (Howe)
This is Howe's showcase acoustic guitar instrumental. It's fine, but probably not strong enough to have escaped the confines of a solo album.

'Don't Take No For An Answer' (Return Trip version only) (Howe)
This was presumably offered up as Howe's lead vocal track to compete with Squire's, but was left off the final version of the 2011 album. I actually rather like the song, but again it sounds like it needs further development and really ought to have stayed on a Howe solo album. It does have some impressive keyboards, presumably from Downes, but the song itself is not quite strong enough in its current form.

'Into the Storm' (Squire, Wakeman, Howe, Horn, David, White)
This rather splendid piece epitomises what the later Yes were still capable of achieving. Up tempo and progressive while keeping the song intact, it was developed during Oliver Wakeman's time in the band, although recorded with Downes firmly in place, who plays the rather catchy synthesiser melody. With a general choral approach to the vocals, the lack of Benoît David in the *Return Trip* version is barely noticed, and the arrangement is left firmly 'as is' in the 2018 version. As an album closer, it is excellent and was played live on the late 2011 tour.

Heaven and Earth (2014)

Personnel:
Jon Davison: vocals, acoustic guitar
Chris Squire: bass, vocals
Steve Howe: electric and acoustic guitars, steel guitar, Portuguese guitar, vocals
Alan White: drums, percussion
Geoff Downes: keyboards, programming
Produced by Roy Thomas Baker at Neptune Studios, Los Angeles.
Mixing and backing vocal recording: Billy Sherwood
Recorded January to March 2014.
Released July 2014
Highest chart places: UK: 20, USA: 26
Running time: 51:29

> We recorded an album of demos.
> Jon Davison, *Yes Music Podcast,* 2023

The band decided to record another album for Frontiers Records, the Italian label best known for its hard rock acts, and went into the studio in the California area in January 2014 to begin work. By this time, David had been replaced by US singer Jon Davison following some health issues for Benoit, for which the band were not prepared to wait. However, there is little doubt that Davison was quite a find for the band. A strong live singer, with a sort of lithe charisma, and a timbre and register close to Anderson but just about far enough away to exist in the right netherworld between imitation and innovation. He has proved to be consistent and adaptable, and not intimidated by the star status of the other members of the band. He was also strongly motivated to write and record new material and in a bizarre move, Roy Thomas Baker – who had overseen the abortive Paris Sessions 35 years before – was brought in as producer, with Billy Sherwood recording and mixing the backing vocals, which were recorded right at the end of the sessions, in March 2014.

After ten weeks in the studio, the band returned to the road and did not revisit the material, something that Howe specifically has suggested was a mistake. There's definitely something missing from the finished article. It may be as simple as attention to detail or indeed, a loving hand on the tiller. It seems to me that a lot of the material is underdeveloped, with some tracks left to drift, in some cases a good two minutes beyond their natural running time. The old band – from any era, even 2011 – would have honed those tracks within inches of their lives. Here the arrangements seem half-hearted, almost like glorified demos, as Davison later confirmed in the quote at the start of this section

But the truth is that *Heaven And Earth* is, at best, a bit of a damp squib of an album. Not that it is awful – there's something on every track that I like

– but it is hard to understand who the album is for, really. Fans expecting 70s-era Yes will be disappointed. So will fans of the Rabin era. It doesn't even have the energy or – more importantly – the clarity of purpose of *Fly From Here,* recorded just three years before. The phrase that comes to mind is 'soft rock'. The songs are pleasant, tuneful and unassuming, but there's no fire and not enough craft.

Furthermore, this was to be Chris Squire's last album before his desperately sad and shocking death in June 2015. In fact, although the rhythm section of Squire and White is hardly the powerhouse it once was on *Heaven and Earth*, his playing – and that of Alan White – is perfectly fine. The tempos, however, really drag on almost every track, falling into a monotonous plod. Fans of the band had been complaining about slowing speeds for some years, but here they are for the first time laid bare on an album. Additionally, Davison is responsible for a shockingly large amount of the material. There's no crime in that, but it does point to a lack of enthusiasm from the rest of the group.

However, there are some bright spots. Howe remains ever the professional, colouring each track with just enough to stave off complete narcolepsy and Geoff Downes also appears to be enjoying himself. But it's not quite enough. While those wanting another *Close To The Edge* may have been over-ambitious, it's not just about musical fire and ambition. There's a lot you can do with arrangements and attention to detail. Here there's very little like that, just some mediocre songs played fairly straight. In the final analysis, while *Open Your Eyes* (for instance) produced a violent reaction against it, *Heaven and Earth* elicited a somewhat mediocre response. Some liked it, others disliked it, but few felt strongly enough about it to love it or hate it, and that's a little bit sad, particularly for Chris Squire.

'Believe Again' (Davison, Howe)

It's not the greatest of starts. 'Believe Again' is light and tuneful, and feels like the sort of song that would be considered filler on an album like *The Ladder*. Some things do work. Davison's lead vocal shows commitment and Squire's harmony vocal is rather splendid. The instrumental section halfway through is mildly arresting, and Downes' synthesiser solo is a nice touch, as is Howe's closing guitar salvo. However, overall it's too low-key for an opening song, and feels just a touch too long for the quality of the material. The first example of an arrangement that might have been tightened considerably. The song was played live on the 2014 tour.

'The Game' (Squire, Davison, Gerard Johnson)

This is rather better. 'The Game' grew from a writing session between Chris Squire and keyboard player Gerard Johnson (The Syn), and while the arrangement could really do with some bite, it's still a good song. Howe's parts are mainly played on the acoustic guitar, although his solos are good, and it all feels a little sparse. The melody suits Davison's voice and the 'pop' backing vocals are nicely done, but again it's a little overlong for what is, essentially, a soft rock tune. Like 'Believe Again', this song was played live on the tour later that year.

'Step Beyond' (Howe, Davidson)

This track flatters to deceive in that it has a perky, catchy synthesiser riff, a decent backing vocal arrangement and some rather more strident guitar. However, the track itself is a rather underwhelming plod – it would certainly have benefitted from a more lively tempo, at times, it's so slow you could make a cup of tea between snare beats.

'To Ascend' (Davison, White)

A lovely, acoustic start – one of the better on the album – leads into a nice song that actually benefits from its sedate pace. Downes is particularly good here – his piano arrangement is excellent. It's hardly a classic, but it's good to hear a different texture. 'To Ascend' was also occasionally played live on the subsequent tour.

'In A World Of Our Own' (Davison, Squire)

Ah, once again, something different – a shuffle, and it's nicely done, although Davison's vocal needs a little more meat – perhaps double-tracking might have helped, and as a result, it all seems a little insipid. Squire's backing vocals are excellent on the rather catchy chorus, and the track has a Beatle-esque swagger that makes it one of the better pieces on the album. Downes, again, comes up with some nice textures, particularly his Hammond riff towards the end of the song, and Howe is excellent. Again, a faster tempo would have been helpful.

'Light Of The Ages' (Davison)

Although Davison has the only writing credit on this track, the opening feels all the world like a Howe solo piece, with pedal steel to the fore. It's Davison on acoustic, here – with Howe on electric – actually sounding rather like his former GTR band-mate Steve Hackett, and here the arrangement is somewhat more ambitious with Squire and Downes both making good contributions. Sadly, the song doesn't quite match the arrangement, although it's good to hear Alan White being tested a little more than previously on the album.

'It Was All We Knew' (Howe)

This Steve Howe composition is one of his better efforts in recent years. It's probably the best-constructed piece on the album, with some great guitar (as you might expect) but also a very fine vocal arrangement. It's hardly innovative, but it's well constructed and played, and on such a mediocre album, that's a real pleasure.

'Subway Walls' (Davison, Downes)

Downes's superb orchestral introduction – with percussive interjections from White – is probably the high point of the album, particularly for old-school Yes fans. There's also some great work from Squire, Downes and White in the main arrangement that gives this track much more of a 'Yes' feel, even if Davison's main melody line is a little insipid. At least you can hear some ambition in this piece. The middle instrumental section – with a powerful organ solo from Downes followed by some great work from Howe – is again a real highlight, and while the album itself may not be the greatest tribute to Chris Squire, this track at least hints at what he was still capable of. The song ends beautifully, with a slow build to a powerful finish. A strong track to close the album and something of a relief.

Related tracks

None, although the Japanese release features an acoustic version of 'To Ascend'.

From A Page (2019)

Personnel:
Chris Squire: Bass and vocals
Steve Howe: Guitar and vocals
Alan White: Drums
Oliver Wakeman: Keyboards and vocals
Benoit David: Lead vocals
Produced by Oliver Wakeman
Engineered by Patrick MacDougall and Tim Weidner
Recorded in Phoenix, Arizona and Beverley Hills, California 2010-2011
Additional keyboards and backing vocals recorded at 'The Opus Suite', UK.
Mixed by Karl Groom at Thin Ice Studios, Virginia Water, UK.
Mastered by Mike Pietrini

With the Howe / White Yes touring, and making noise about a new studio
album, that such an album as *From A Page* should appear out of the blue
towards the end of 2019, was a shock to many people. The instigator was
Oliver Wakeman, who was in possession of the recordings that the band had
made at the start of the sessions that would become *Fly From Here*. Oliver,
of course, was soon to be replaced by Geoff Downes, and with Trevor Horn
producing, the material was to take on a different character. It was certainly
well known that writing and indeed some recording had taken place before
Oliver's replacement, as is evidenced by some of the pieces that remained
on *Fly From Here* – 'Hour Of Need' being the obvious example. It is also
understandable, in the circumstances, that the tracks that Oliver had largely
written on his own should have been discarded at the time.

What was less known, however, is how much recording had taken place
on some of these tracks. Following Chris' death, Oliver retrieved the files
– initially to work on 'The Gift Of Love' – and pieced them together into
a listenable state. He then went on to work on two more pieces: 'To The
Moment' and 'Words On A Page'. After they had spotted a post on Twitter
about these pieces, he was contacted by the current Yes management, who
suggested he meet up with Steve to discuss a possible release. With Messrs.
Howe and (later) White on board, Oliver continued the process of making
the pieces releasable with the help of Karl Groom at Thin Ice Studios. To
the three Yes tracks, he added a piano version of the song 'From The Turn
Of A Card', sung by Benoit on Oliver's excellent album with Gordon Giltrap,
Ravens And Lullabies.

The justification for this inclusion was that the song had existed as a
demo while Oliver had been in Yes. Indeed, he played it to the band at
the time. The resulting mini-album was released at the end of 2019 via
online progressive rock retailer Burning Shed. It was packaged – slightly
controversially – with a reissue of the Benoit David / Oliver Wakeman-era live
album *In The Present – Live From Lyons*. While this reissue of the live album

itself only included one extra track that had not been on the previous release, from Steve Howe's acoustic set, as a package, they do represent a decent summary of the Oliver era. A wider release was also planned, but, at the time of writing, it had not yet appeared, although there has been a vinyl version and the album can now be heard on streaming sites.

There is a philosophical issue here. The contributions from the four other members at the time, are a little spartan. There's certainly less guitar than might have been expected, although Steve's palate still remains pretty broad. With Oliver having added some keyboards and backing vocals much later, these tracks may well be more keyboard-heavy than they would have been had they been fully developed by all five members of the band. This is not necessarily a bad thing; however, and it has to be said that the final results are very satisfying indeed. There's little doubt that all the songs are ahead of anything on *Heaven And Earth*. Indeed, it could be argued that they are an improvement over many of the pieces on *Fly From Here* outside the main, Horn / Downes-composed suite. The tracks also demonstrate what a loss Oliver was to the band in terms of his songwriting and playing, even if he does get close to his father at times in terms of style.

So, is this, in the end, Yes? Most definitely.

'To The Moment' (Oliver Wakeman)

The first thing to say about 'To The Moment' is that it's a terrific, up-tempo song with one of Yes finest choruses of the new millennium. It's also beautifully sung by Benoit, although his vocals sit a little further back in the mix than on *Fly From Here*. It's also great to hear the distinctive vocals of Chris Squire (and also Steve Howe if I'm not mistaken). This would have been a worthy addition to the 2011 album, and it's wonderful that it has finally appeared. Indeed, Benoit's vocal line is very like something Jon Anderson might have sung, without the Canadian himself sounding like a carbon copy.

One suspects some 'writing to style' from Oliver, but here it really works. It also demonstrates that one of the tragedies of the ousting of Benoit from the band is that he was developing such a character of his own as a vocalist.

There's no doubt that – despite some great and quite hard-rocking lead work from Steve – this is all quite keyboard-heavy, with Oliver channelling his father throughout the track, including a great Moog solo towards the end and some impressive organ swirls. One suspects that more guitars might have been planned but never recorded and some of the rest of the instrumentation feels a touch untidy or mistimed in places. But these are minor quibbles. It's a fantastic start.

'Words On A Page' (Oliver Wakeman)

This song starts beautifully – acoustic guitar and piano combining with great charm in this quieter piece. Benoit's lead vocal is tender and the vocal melody is lilting; it's once again quite Anderson-like. Oliver's piano is the star, as the guitar takes more of a back seat in the verses, before returning in the lengthy instrumental section, heralding an electric solo which first expresses the main melody and then plays with it. The final vocal reprise – with Benoit singing in counterpoint to what sounds like Oliver's own backing vocals – is also very effective. While this track is slighter in character than the opener and rather more in keeping with the somewhat more sentimental, latter-day version of the band, the bar is again kept pretty high in terms of quality.

'From The Turn Of A Card' (Oliver Wakeman)
While this isn't really Yes at all, it's a charming diversion that helps bring balance to this four-track mini-album. It features Benoit's vocal performance of the song from Oliver's album with Gordon Giltrap, *Ravens And Lullabies*. With that full band performance replaced by piano, this rather lovely song works nicely, although checking out the original version is highly recommended, as indeed is the rest of that excellent album.

'The Gift Of Love' (Wakeman, Squire, Howe, David, White)
Where would we be without an epic on a Yes album, and here it is. We begin with a wash of keyboards, with Oliver's lead synths to the fore, before the rest of the band enter for the first verse and chorus, with Chris' lead vocal on the chorus movingly high in the mix. Steve's guitar is more prominent in the second vocal section, and much of the rest of the piece is dependent on the repetition of a six-note refrain, with the band varying the arrangement around it. Steve contributes some fine lead guitar, and there's an unexpected and distinctive piano solo as the piece builds to its conclusion.

While this all works very in context and once again can compare very favourably with anything on *Heaven And Earth*, it does stretch what is essentially a single idea a long way. The piece's tempo also drags a little, as so many of the tracks on that later album did. Additionally, the arrangement feels spartan in places, and again one suspects some more guitar might have lifted things a little. So, 'The Gift Of Love' is probably the least successful track of the three, but it's still a fine achievement.

The Quest (2021)

Personnel:
Jon Davison: lead and backing vocals, acoustic guitar
Steve Howe: electric and acoustic guitars, Portuguese 12 string guitar, Pedal Steel, mandolin, koto, lead and backing vocals
Geoff Downes: keyboards
Billy Sherwood: bass guitar, keyboards, acoustic guitar, lead and backing vocals
Alan White: drums
Additional musicians:
Jay Schellen: percussion
FAMES Studio Orchestra
Paul K. Joyce: orchestra arrangements
Oleg Kondratenko: conductor
Produced by Steve Howe
Engineering and mixing by Curtis Schwartz
Mastered by Simon Heyworth
Released 1 October 2021 (UK and Europe)
Highest chart places: UK: 20, Aus: 14, USA: Did not chart

During the latter half of the 2010s – following the death of Chris Squire in 2015 – Yes had largely become a touring outfit, slugging it out for audiences for a while with Yes featuring ARW. However, the release of the well-received, surprise mini-album *From A Page* showed that there was still some appetite for new Yes music – although, at the time of writing, that album still hadn't had a full, physical, standalone release, appearing instead on streaming services later in 2020.

   In late 2019, it became apparent that a new album from the current lineup of the official band might be in the works. Indeed, some initial ideas were floating around between the band well before the coronavirus epidemic, which put a stop to live touring for two years, took hold of the world in early 2020. With outside producers considered, at best, a double-edged sword, Steve Howe himself was elected to produce the album, working very much as an ideas hub, in the sort of role that Trevor Horn or Bruce Fairbairn might have enjoyed earlier in Yes' career, rather than an 'engineering' producer that (for instance) Billy Sherwood might have been. Technical backup was given by Curtis Schwartz at his studio in Sussex, UK.

   During 2020, with each musician working remotely but with Howe and Davison (who travelled to the UK, before moving there permanently), built on the ideas presented by each musician. Sherwood, working in California, recorded his own bass and keyboard parts along with White's drums. Indeed, that White played all the drums on the album was considered something of a surprise given the ill health over the previous few years that had stopped him from performing as much part as he would like in live shows. Live drummer Jay Schellen played percussion on several tracks.

Mixing took place in Sussex in the spring of 2021, with Howe and Schwarz at the helm.

Crucially, the band changed recording label for this new outing. Thomas Waber's Inside Out label was a natural fit for the band, given that the label also had old stagers like Steve Hackett on its roster. Inside Out, however, do things in a very specific way. In particular, they tend to release albums in many different formats, with vinyl editions now essential, but also deluxe collector's editions and bluray versions – enough for any hardened Yes fan with money in their pockets. It was also Inside Out that wisely suggested the band release the main album with around 50 minutes of music, with a 'special edition' providing a further three songs from the sessions. A superb, eye-catching Roger Dean cover was considered essential, and the veteran artist turned in an excellent painting in his 'fantastical landscape' style. A further link to the 1970s band was provided when it was revealed that three of the tracks would have 'sections' in the same way that pieces like 'And You and I' had in the 1970s. Whether these named sections were really necessary or an affectation to please long-term fans, only the band and label can say, but to call the final solo section of 'The Ice Bridge' 'Interaction', for instance, seems to be stating the obvious – it's a duet featuring lead guitar and lead synth.

What, then, would the album sound like? There seemed to be several schools of thought when fans compiled their sonic wish lists. Firstly, it was hoped that the album would sound nothing like *Heaven and Earth* – considered (with some exceptions) unsatisfactory by fans and even the band themselves. Secondly, some commentators – as they always do – hoped that this would be a return to 'classic Yes', last attempted in earnest with *Magnification* more than 20 years previously. Others, however, including your author, hoped that the five musicians would produce the best music they could create as a unit, regardless of tone or style.

When 'The Ice Bridge' was released as the first video track from the album on 23 July 2021, it seemed that the 'classic Yes' camp might win the day. Here was an eight-minute piece with an angular, progressive tone, a guitar/synth duet and little by way of a traditional 'song'. Some were delighted, others underwhelmed. Some even fretted that this was an attempt to pastiche the sound of classic 1970s Yes.

Furthermore, within a few days, a problem emerged. The piece had largely been put together by Geoff Downes, who had found a demo of the music on a tape of music originally written as 'library' music in 1977. Downes, understandably, thought he had written the track himself, but it quickly transpired that the music had, in fact, been composed by former Curved Air and Sky keyboard player Francis Monkman. This genuine mistake was quickly corrected amicably, but it did allow those with a less than favourable view of the current lineup to shout 'told you so' for a while. Monkman was, sadly, to die in 2023.

The use of an orchestra on several tracks was also seen as a link back to past glories – having first been tried by the band in 1970 on *Time and a Word*, and further developed as an idea on Magnification and on the subsequent tour in 2001.

The album was finally released on 1 October 2021 to a decent reception. As it turned out, 'The Ice Bridge' was something of an outlier, with most of the album taking on a rather more laid back character – not quite sounding like Yes, but not quite sounding like anyone else either. Some early reviewers bemoaned the lack of the band's traditional creativity, Geoff Barton in *Classic Rock* calling it 'twee and unchallenging' and querying why the three bonus tracks were on a separate disc when there was plenty of room to include them on the main one, while Chris Roberts in *Prog* was a little more positive, suggesting that there were 'flashes of the old magic'. Slightly more broadminded fans generally gave it a thumbs up and sales were good, with the album peaking at a creditable 20 in the UK and number seven in Germany, although it didn't chart in the USA.

In terms of the music, despite the nods to the Yes of old, there are some important differences. Excepting on the robust 'The Ice Bridge', Downes' keyboards are relatively subdued – closer to his role in Asia. It's Howe's guitar textures – and there are certainly plenty of them – that dominate. Furthermore, there had been a change in emphasis on the vocal front. There were now three lead vocalists in the band, with Sherwood and Howe both taking on enhanced vocal roles, whether as occasional lead vocalists or in providing a richer tonal variation in the backing and harmony vocals. With Chris Squire much missed, this change in sonic balance works surprisingly well, with Howe's deeper voice never better exploited. Elsewhere, Alan White sets aside his recent health issues to deliver a solid performance, even if the relative simplicity of the material means that his dexterity (or lack thereof) is rarely tested.

Despite the red herring that is 'The Ice Bridge', the album does not attempt to recall past glories but represents the creative ambitions of Howe, Davison, Sherwood and Downes (less so White) as they existed during the writing and recording process. It strikes me as being an 'honest' album – an attempt to create without preconceptions, although it does feel 'middle-aged' – in a good way. None of its creators, after all, are young men, and they are not making music with the fire and energy of musicians in their 20s. Instead, this is a well-produced and crafted collection of pieces and a massive advance over *Heaven and Earth*. Whether the listener likes what they hear, it's impossible not to admire the construction and thought that has gone into these songs. Indeed, the album is often genuinely moving.

'The Ice Bridge' i. 'Eyes East' ii. 'Race Against Time' iii. 'Interaction'
(Davison, Monkman, Downes)
A synth fanfare opens the album in rousing style. This is the track that got some fans excited at the prospect of a return to 1970s-style Yes, and it's not

hard to see why. Downes' keyboards are prominent, as is Howe's languid lead guitar, while Davison's vocal section has the distinct feel of Anderson in its angular melody. Indeed, Sherwood's bass dances in a very Squire-like fashion.

And yet, one wonders if the 1970s band would have attempted anything as – frankly – obvious as this, particularly in the way that Downes' (or perhaps Monkman's) second fanfare sounds more like the theme for a TV game show than a piece of vintage progressive rock. That said, the final duet between synth and guitar, based around Howe's repetitive yet catchy riff, is impressively done and the environmentalist lyrics are very evocative: 'all eyes to the east'. This is somewhat prescient considering that, as I write these words, Russia is at war with Ukraine ...

Overall, it's an impressive opening track, even if it doesn't represent the tone of the rest of the album. It was played live during the band's 2022 live dates.

'Dare To Know' (Howe)

Released as the second video track before the release of the album, 'Dare To Know' is another piece with hints of earlier incarnations of the band, although it's the *Magnification* version of Yes that is most referenced here. On this occasion, however, the use of the orchestra doesn't inhibit either Howe –who is the star here on his own song – or Downes, who contributes some pleasing organ. The other main feature of the track is Howe's voice, providing a well-judged contrast to Davison, with Howe singing an octave lower; a pleasing effect. Overall, it's a lovely piece, a little aimless possibly, but strong melodically, and the orchestral arrangement is delightfully well-judged.

'Minus The Man' (Davison, Sherwood)

Sherwood gets his first writing credit here, and this song is rather lovely, with another strong guitar motif from Howe and a lilting vocal melody. Sherwood's penchant for very close-harmony vocals, which can be heard on many of his solo recordings and which can feel cluttered when overused, thankfully, works exceptionally well as a nice variation in approach. Davison and Sherwood's voices work beautifully together and the orchestra is unobtrusive, although, on this track, Downes is largely replaced by the strings. Sherwood's bass playing – especially as the song lifts in intensity in its second half – is exceptional.

'Leave Well Alone' i. 'Across The Border' ii. 'Not For Nothing' iii. 'Wheels' (Howe)

Yes get funky with a Koto? Well, they certainly do for the early part of this lengthy piece, another Howe solo write. The Japanese instrument carries the main riff as the track gets underway, punctuated by synth fanfares. The piece changes tone into an initial vocal section, again shared by Davison and Howe, with the latter perhaps the lead voice here. It's an impressive start – they actually sound uncannily like Simon and Garfunkel. Acoustic textures give way to electric ones and a return to the initial theme. That there are multiple sections hints at the Yes of old, of course, but actually, it's all a bit stop-start, a slightly clunky arrangement. The final instrumental section, 'Wheels' plods rather when it might have been a good opportunity for the piece to soar, despite a lengthy and jaunty solo from Howe. It's all fine, but perhaps the least successful piece on the main eight-song album, and the most like a Howe solo track – a gripe of many correspondents in the weeks after release.

'The Western Edge' (Davison, Sherwood)
Nominally starting 'side two' is the excellent 'The Western Edge' – a call for global unity. Davison and Sherwood share vocals here, with Sherwood singing some lead and this works wonderfully well, as does some thumping synth.

Better still, after a mid-paced opening, the song has moments of genuine pace, something rare on Yes albums in the 21st century. There are moments of over-complication in the way the vocals are delivered, but these never grate, and this is one song on the album that might have benefitted from a longer running time.

'Future Memories' (Davison)
Davison's love song is very successful. Though initially, it doesn't feel very Yes-like, there's plenty of precedent for pieces with a strong dose of romanticism in Yes, from the much-loved 'Onward' from *Tormato* to the much-derided 'Circus of Heaven' from the same album, via 'Sweetness' and even 'And You and I'. The initial guitar introduction is played by Davison himself, and the verses are pensive and edgy, with pedal guitar from Howe before resolving into a somewhat sappy but delightfully melodic chorus; its sentiment is simple but well-judged.

'Music To My Ears' (Howe)
Downes comes into his own with some tasteful piano and Mellotron on this Howe-penned song, with Davison and Howe once again singing the lead vocal in unison. It's simple stuff with a catchy, repetitive chorus and a nice vocal arrangement. It's perhaps a touch too catchy, so causing some commentators to cry 'twee' and it could certainly do with a bit more pace since the rockier middle eight almost crawls to a halt. But, to quote Douglas Adams, it's 'mostly harmless'.

'A Living Island' i. 'Brave The Storm' ii. 'Wake Up' iii. 'We Will Remember' (Davison, Downes)
The band leave the best for last, without doubt, with this emotive and beautifully constructed piece of music. In truth, this is not 'Yes music' as Jon Anderson might define it. It comes from a slightly different tradition, mixing folk with soft rock, but it's superb nonetheless. Davison meditates on being

locked down during the coronavirus pandemic of 2020 with his partner. Whereas 'Future Memories' was a touch sappy, here he gets the tone just right, allowing the instrumentation – in particular, Downes' superb keyboard arrangement – to tug at the heartstrings naturally. On 'A Living Island' they get it exactly right, arriving at a sort of alternative, rather more gentle style of progressive rock that really works. To these ears, this is Yes' finest moment post-Anderson and a rousing way to end the main album.

Bonus Tracks

As mentioned, new label Inside Out do like a bit of added value, and so special editions of *The Quest* included three additional tracks on a different disc that were recorded for the album but wisely left out of the final selection. As a group of songs, these are lightweight – probably too lightweight – and lack the quality of the main album. There are some decent tunes across the fourteen minutes of these tracks, of course, and nothing is less than competent. But it was a smart move to preserve the integrity of the main disc since they do not have the quality or depth of the pieces on the main album.

'Sister Sleeping Soul' (Davison, Howe)

Some excellent bass work from Sherwood redeems this relatively nondescript song. Howe provides some nice mandolin work, and the vocal arrangement is pleasing, as is a rather decent synth solo from Downes. But the core song is lightweight and substandard. It's unlikely to make many playlists, one feels.

'Mystery Song' (Howe)

Beatles tributes and pastiches are a bit of a cliché, and this one – good-natured though it is – is tolerable at best. Howe's lyrics are affectionate but a touch trite, though his lead guitar is charming. But overall, this is a piece of slightly grating fluff and the worst piece of the eleven presented across the two discs.

'Damaged World' (Howe)

Downes here again gets an enhanced role with some fine synth work – it's a shame that some of his best work on the album is banished to these less impressive bonus tracks. Otherwise, this is a Howe lead vocal, recalling some of his slightly less impressive efforts on his solo albums, with backup from Davison, and it's a pleasantly jaunty piece, perhaps the best of the three here.

Mirror To The Sky (2023)

Personnel:
Jon Davison: lead vocals, acoustic guitar
Steve Howe: guitars, steel, vocals
Geoff Downes: keyboards
Billy Sherwood: bass guitar, vocals
Jay Schellen: drums, percussion
FAMES Studio Orchestra
Paul K. Joyce: orchestra arrangements
Oleg Kondratenko: conductor
Produced by Steve Howe
Engineering and mixing by Curtis Schwartz
Mastered by Simon Heyworth
Chart places: UK: 30. US: 22
Running time: 63:35

As soon as *The Quest* was released, Howe announced that the band were already at work on another album. The sad death of Alan White in 2022 did not really hold things up particularly. Schellen was originally drafted in as a replacement on the band's 2022 tour celebrating the 50th anniversary of *Close To The Edge*, but White passed away before it began. It had been a surprise to many that White had managed to play the drums on *The Quest*, and it was a logical step that Jay Schellen should take over. He was officially confirmed as the band's permanent replacement in 2023, to zero surprise from anyone

While the personnel that were involved in the album, from Engineer Curtis Schwartz to orchestral arranger Paul K. Joyce remained the same, tonally, the album offered plenty of differences. Here, it would seem, would be a return to long-form pieces with two tracks at around nine minutes, and the title track clocking in at almost fourteen.

Early reports considered the album a 'return to form' (often the kiss of death), with *Prog* magazine, for instance, heralding the album as 'The best Yes album in 20 years'. Meanwhile, comments in the fan community were somewhat more mixed. Predictably, those that were ill-disposed to what some called 'The Steve Howe Band' hated the album. On the other hand, there was a certain level of defensiveness amongst some who defended the current lineup, suggesting almost that as the band were producing long-form pieces again, it was almost the duty of Yes fans to love the album. In truth, all that can be expected of Yes fans is to give the album a fair listen and judge it on its own merits. Music is a completely subjective art form. It either moves the listener or it doesn't. No music has a God-given right to be liked.

So, do we like this latest album? Yes, we do, but with reservations.

In terms of individual performance, it's good to hear Steve Howe stretching himself sonically (if not technically, these days). It's a far more 'electric' album than the one that preceded it, with a lot – possibly too much

– pedal steel. Jon Davison sings and writes well, with some suitably 'Yes-like' lyrics. His vocals rarely have the rock edge of Anderson, but the music adapts to that. Schellen is solid but unspectacular, while Sherwood's bass is exceptional, although his other contributions (save his writing talents) are largely missing. He supplies a few lines of lead vocal, but Howe's voice remains more prominent. The older man's singing remains much improved but an acquired taste. As for Downes, the decision to use mainly vintage keys is an interesting one, yet Downes's mastery is texture – mainly of a digital nature – and his better contributions are once again banished to the bonus tracks. His writing – he only contributes one co-write on the worst track on the album – is much missed.

Whereas *The Quest* felt a little disjointed as an album, with the bad seemingly working in small groups or as individuals before adding contributions to the rest of the band, as individual pieces, the songs worked well. *Mirror To The Sky* genuinely feels like the band are more integrated and working as a unit. Some of the material is also strong. And yet, some of it isn't and the way that various motifs and sections are placed into the longer songs sometimes seems random and without obvious structure. Again, this is a band pointing backwards to their 'classic' years but not quite hitting the mark. If *The Quest* was a transition to a 'new' Yes, then *Mirror To The Sky* hits the breaks somewhat and points back again in a way that is both frustrating and hopeful. If the band keeps recording – and it looks like it will – it could well be that it produces music in the future that, while not reaching the creative and energetic heights of their early 1970s peak, at least hints at past glories.

'Cut From The Stars' (Davison, Sherwood)
Trailed ahead of the full album, this opener is terrific. It manages to be both hook-laden and a bit hard to get into. This is due to the song's unusual structure and the way its various motifs – all excellent – drop in and out. After a burst of strings, 'lifted' from later in the piece, It jogs a long at a very decent pace, interspersed with some rather more pensive sections, with some superb bass from Sherwood. Howe uses an unusual tone here, and Downes' conributions are some of his best on the album, based around organ and electric piano. The track ends on a little duet between Howe and Downes, this time on Moog. It's all catchy and beautifully judged. A great, breathless start.

'All Connected' (Davison, Howe, Sherwood)
This nine-minute piece starts very promisingly, with a multi-structured instrumental section featuring Howe at his most eclectic. Again, the pace is decent as the vocals enter, though Davison is here mixed a little low for comfort. Sherwood's counterpoint vocal is also welcome. Three and a half minutes in, however, we have several different sections thrown at us that never develop, and for the rest of the piece, they come at us in what feels

like a random pattern. They are all beautifully constructed, but it's ironic, given the title of the song, that they don't really feel connected at all. It remains – to these ears – an interesting but frustrating listen, despite Howe's fine pedal steel coda.

'Luminosity' (Davison, Howe, Sherwood)
'Luminosity' opens with an impressive, if low-energy instrumental passage that might have come from a Howe solo album before resolving into the main 'song', which has an initial melody that stays just the right side of 'Hey nonny nonny' cheese before developing into a far more impressive piece, punctuated by Moog arpeggios from Downes. Sherwood's bass is pleasingly un-Squire-like. It's all fine and tuneful, if a bit underwhelming. The last three minutes are devoted to an extended pedal steel solo, with a chord structure that feels like the closing moments of 'Ritual' without having any of that song's intensity. These last three minutes are – arguably – superfluous.

'Living Out Their Dream' (Howe, Downes)
This is the obligatory short 'rawk' song on the album, and it's another psych / Beatle pastiche (if not quite as obvious as the ones on *The Quest*) which works reasonably well, with Davison and Howe's voices in unison. Howe makes some unfortunate tone choices, and it passes in a pleasant if entirely forgettable manner. Howe's extended solo from three minutes in is the highlight of an otherwise underwhelming track.

'Mirror To The Sky' (Davison, Howe)
So, to the much heralded and long-awaited 14-minute title track. It certainly grabs the attention from the off, as, from the first moments, we seem to be in the Mississippi Delta, with Howe's heavily reverbed, solo intro, before Downes joins in with some 'Video Killed The Radio Star'-style piano chords. The initial band section is terrific -bold, powerful and, once again, benefitting from some superb, funky bass from Sherwood. The next couple of minutes are the boldest, most progressive Yes music since *Magnification.*

The pace slows, with Howe and Davison repeatedly telling us of 'Dreams of a sky without fire' joined by the orchestra. The track then slips back into the overall tone of the other longer tracks – tuneful if low-energy. It's all lovely but lacking in the intensity of the best Yes music. We admire it, but we do not thrill to this music. The main song drifts along for another five minutes before a slower instrumental section does grab the attention, then a powerful intervention from the orchestra leads into an all too brief reiteration of the opening section and a big finish.

This epic flatters to deceive. When it thrills, it does so in spades, but it does get bogged down in its middle six minutes in a song section that is decent enough but loses the intensity of the track's early instrumental section.

'Circles Of Time' (Davison)
There is a grand tradition of Yes closing pieces. These are either epics (think 'Heart Of The Sunrise') or 'coda' pieces such as 'Nine Voices' (good) or 'Holy Lamb' (horrible). This one falls into the latter category in terms of style not quality. Even though it's over five minutes long, it's a good 'un, thankfully. It's a charmingly naive song from Davison, featuring his own acoustic guitar, with help from Howe and the orchestra. It's tuneful and – unlike a few pieces on the album -doesn't overstay its welcome in an effort to appear 'epic'. It's a beautiful closer.

Bonus Tracks
As with *The Quest, Mirror* has a second disc containing three songs, all written by Steve Howe. They are all somewhat better than their equivalents on *The Quest*, too. Interestingly, there's a 'live' feel to these pieces, as less time has been spent on instrumental complexity, so they genuinely feel like they've been played by 'band'. That said, they also feel like Steve Howe solo tracks in many ways, although if they did indeed appear on one, we'd probably be remarking how good they were!

'Unknown Place' (Howe)
This is the longest of the three bonus tracks, and is based around a descending riff played by Howe and Sherwood. A lengthy instrumental section includes some wonderful Hammond work from Downes. At five minutes, the track takes a sudden turn into a classical guitar and church organ passage, before a final vocal section ends the piece. This is pretty good – the up-tempo instrumental section is one of the most satisfying on the album. It's a shame the rest of the track is so unfocused, relatively speaking. But as bonus tracks go, it's very decent.

'One Second Is Enough' (Howe)
More organ introduces another descending riff from Howe, who takes the lead vocal in unison with Davison. The pre-chorus instrumental motif is disconcertingly catchy, as is the chorus itself. It's all very pleasant and very lightweight but has genuine charm.

'Magic Potion' (Howe)
Yet another song based around a Howe guitar motif, but with another funky bassline from Sherwood, Howe again shares vocals with Davison. Once again, it's quite catchy and lightweight, passing by pleasantly, but without any of the depth we associate with Yes.

Epilogue – Yes Enter Their Sixth Decade

The death of Chris Squire in 2015 led to an inevitable weakening of the central Yes 'brand' in the eyes of many (but by no means all) fans of the band. Chris' death was untimely, as was Alan White's, who left us in 2022 after several years of poor health, to be replaced by his understudy of several years, Jay Schellen. Only Steve Howe – very sprightly in his 70s – represents the most innovative years of the band's history, and while he doesn't seem able to play at full capacity, he has adapted his style and he remains a very fine guitarist. The band has also seen other Yes alumni make guest appearances with Tony Kaye, Patrick Moraz and Trevor Horn (who sang 'Tempus Fugit' at several British concerts in 2016 and 2018). The role of Peter Banks in the development of the group and who died in 2013 – has also been acknowledged by the band, especially Howe.

Following the 50th birthday celebrations in 2018, live activity came to a halt with the Covid 19 pandemic. The band had been trailering – for what seemed like an eternity – concerts in which they were to play the whole of *Relayer*. These were set aside in 2022 while the 50th anniversary of *Close To The Edge* was celebtrated, in decent performances, which also saw a couple of songs from *The Quest* played. *Relayer* was postponed to 2023, and when those concerts in Europe were abandoned due to the lack of availability of adequate post-Covid insurance, the *Relayer* idea was dropped completely, to some consternation from long-suffering fans.

The current lineup also continues to meet opposition from a stubborn but very vocal section of their fanbase. Davison, it is argued, is just a weak Anderson imitator. Downes is not a patch on the Wakeman family. (NB. Don't let the naysayers fool you. Downes may not be able to let rip a Moog solo like Wakeman or Moraz, but he's possibly the band's most innovative musician).

Meanwhile, there was Yes-related activity outside the official band. It was first announced that Jon Anderson, Trevor Rabin and Rick Wakeman were working on new music together in 2010. Wakeman and Anderson had toured together as a duo and had also produced a modest, low-key album in *The Living Tree*. However, a tour – with notorious manager Brian Lane co-ordinating – commenced in the USA in late 2016 and Europe in March 2017. The band featured two musicians well known to Wakeman – bassist Lee Pomeroy, and to Rabin – drummer Lou Molinaro III. The band were more ambitious than the Howe lineup – choosing larger venues to play. A second tour to celebrate the 50th anniversary took place in 2018. By 2017, the band had added 'Yes' to their moniker, calling themselves Yes featuring Jon Anderson, Trevor Rabin and Rick Wakeman. Musically the setlist was the inevitable hybrid of Rabin era and Wakeman era material, including several tracks from *90125*, but also pieces like 'Awaken' and 'And You And I'. Both bands existed in an uneasy truce for a while.

But ARW was to be short-lived. While Anderson and Wakeman had hoped to reconvene the band at some point, Rabin finally put paid to any hopes of this in an interview in *Prog Magazine* in April 2020. Indeed, both he and Wakeman had also been highly critical of the move to call the band 'Yes' in the first place.

Post Covid, however, Anderson and both Rick and Oliver Wakeman have been busy with Yes-related projects. Oliver looks set to play his Yes mini-album *From A Page* for the first time in 2023 with the organisational assistance of your author. Anderson – still very sprightly in his late 70s – has convened several different bands to play Yes material, touring with both the Paul Green Rock Academy and The Band Geeks, the latter playing authentic arrangements of Yes classics. Rick Wakeman continues to play live with The English Rock Ensemble. He has always played 'Starship Trooper', but his live shows now contain a wider range of Yes material. Horn even plays 'Owner of a Lonely Heart' in his own live shows. 2023 and 2024 will see Howe's Yes, Anderson and both Rick and Oliver playing live, performing Yes material. It seems that while there is only one Yes, there remain several other units with every right to play Yes material.

It can't go on forever. Anderson, Howe and Rick Wakeman are all in their 70, as are Moraz, Kaye and Downes. Bruford retired more than a dozen years ago. Rabin, Davison, Sherwood and Shellen are younger by only 10 to 20 years. Even Oliver has just turned 50.

So, despite this little flurry of activity, it seems that even these versions of Yes will stop before long. Talk of 'passing the torch' to a younger generation of musicians, with Yes music becoming 'repertoire' seems fanciful but might still happen. More likely, the band will stop at some point and there will be no physical version of Yes. But we'll always have the music. And the memories.

Compilations and Video Biographies

Given the huge amount of solo and live material out there – some of it not of the best quality – the amount of Yes-related compilation albums (particularly of the 'Friends and Relatives' type) released over the years has been staggering. It would be possible – though not much fun – to list them all, but it's more useful to list those releases that at least have some sort of official or semi-official status to them.

Yesterdays (LP, CD, streaming) 1974

This was a stopgap release, a best-of culled from the band's first two albums. As well as six tracks that had appeared on *Yes* and *Time and a Word*, it also included 'Dear Father' – then a rare B-side – and the full, 1972 arrangement of 'America', featuring Bruford, Howe and Wakeman. It's also got a slightly risqué cover from Roger Dean. At the time, it was pretty much an essential purchase, and I do indeed have copies on vinyl and CD, but with both the tracks that were originally unavailable only here now widely available elsewhere, it's now something of a 'completists only' purchase.

Classic Yes (LP, CD, streaming) 1981

Classic Yes is a single album by numbers 'best' of with an attractive Roger Dean cover. Some editions came with a seven-inch single with two live tracks from the *Tormato* tour 'Roundabout' in Oakland and 'I've Seen All Good People' at Wembley. Neither tracks are available elsewhere but are available on the streaming versions of the album. The other tracks are all – of course – fabulous, but this is very much a compilation for the curious, not the fan.

Yesyears and Yes – Greatest Video Hits (VHS, later DVD) 1991

Around the time of the 1991 *Union* tour, Eagle Vision released two videos. The first was *Yesyears*, a two-hour documentary with some live moments, presenting a diplomatic history of the band using testimony from the eight-man *Union* lineup. It's pretty uncritical, is missing some crucial players – like Banks and Moraz – and hardly mentions the *Drama* era or ABWH at all.

The Greatest Video Hits is more fun – official videos and a few live cuts with jokey commentary filmed at one (or more) or the *Union* arena shows. Kaye and Wakeman are the main ringleaders, though Bruford and Rabin are also good value.

Yesyears (4 CD set) 1991

At the same time as the videos above, Atco released a sumptuous four-CD boxed set, showcasing a new logo (which didn't really 'take') and a terrific full-colour programme-style brochure with a band history. It is mainly a best-of, with a few interesting additional or alternative versions, particularly from the Rabin era. It includes two live tracks, which come from 1988 on the *Big*

Generator tour, and do give us the opportunity to hear what sort of fist Tony Kaye makes of 'And You and I' and 'Heart of the Sunrise' (answer – pretty decent). Overall, it is an invaluable, beautifully packaged set for fans and well worth picking up.

In a Word (5 CD set) 2002

To coincide with the Rhino re-master programme, this excellent five CD set – with decent sleeve notes as small essays by a variety of writers – also has a fair few bonus tracks, mainly from the 1979 Paris Sessions, and even features a couple of tracks from the Anderson, Bruford, Wakeman, Howe album. Although the bonus tracks are less interesting than on *Yesyears*, it is still a decent package.

The Ultimate Yes – 35th Anniversary Collection. (2 CD set), 2003

This two-CD set is a different beast – a compilation aimed at the curious non-fan. It actually charted in the UK, and it's a reasonable enough 'starter pack', with a track from every album except *Drama* and the long-form nature of the band represented by 'Ritual' and 'Awaken'. For some reason, however, the version of 'And You and I' is the lesser 'alternative version' from the Rhino re-master of *Close to the Edge* – presumably an error – and a bad one. Chris Welch's sleeve notes are full of rock clichés rather than any sort of proper analysis. If you are reading this book, you probably won't need it.

Yes Remixes (CD) 2003

Now here's a curiosity. In 2003, Virgil Howe – the son of Steve Howe, who tragically died in 2017 – re-imagined ten Yes pieces from between 1970 and 1980. First of all, there's a technical misnomer here. These are not remixes since Virgil clearly had no access to the master tapes. What he did do was add beats, keyboards and some other instrumentation to segments of existing Yes songs to give each of them a different texture within the 'techno' genre. If that sounds awful, well – surprisingly – it isn't. Virgil, AKA The Verge, was clever, sometimes repeating small riffs or instrumental sections, even layering other sections from the same song over the top. More often than not, this works pretty well, the highlight being a gloriously lovely 'chill out' take on 'Ritual'.

Elsewhere, the results are quirkier, although never less than interesting, with whole sections of the original songs retained in some cases. The album finishes with 'No Clowns', less techno, more 'Revolution No.9'-style sound collage, featuring many Yes pieces including, as you might guess, 'Circus Of Heaven'.

Yes – Their definitive Fully Authorized Story (2 x DVD) Classic Artists. 2008

Far better and more revealing than *Yesyears*, this is a far less homogenised version of the Yes story. As well as the main band, it also pulls in other correspondents like long-time supporter Phil Carson, Peter Banks and the *Drama* period is not ignored this time out. It's far more honest, although some crucial talking heads are still missing – Like Brian Lane and Patrick Moraz. But as a largely warts and all summary of the story to date, it's not at all bad.

Live Recordings – on CD and DVD

If you are reading this book, you are probably already aware of the large amount of Yes live material that has been released over the years. Yes are not the only band to have huge amounts of such material, of course. The King Crimson camp, for instance, with Robert Fripp at the helm, have put out many live recordings, while other bands – Pearl Jam spring to mind – have taken great pleasure in releasing many different live shows – often from the same tour.

There has been little structure to what had been released in the band's name over the years. We will discuss the 'official' output, pre-1990, in a moment. There are many bootlegs – of varying quality – from the years when live recording was an expensive business. In the modern era, however, the need for bootlegs has been scuppered by a slew of live recordings – of almost every tour. Indeed, Yes have even tapped into the fashion – now falling out of favour, it would seem – of offering live renditions of that very night's show, either via download or via CD.

One might well ask – how many live versions of 'Heart of the Sunrise' do I need? I have eight live versions on my iPod right now, and that is far from comprehensive. I still play the studio version far more often than any of these live recordings. On the other hand, there are Yes fans that pour over the subtleties of individual parts and performances, and that's fine. One of the things that makes Yes so fascinating is the variation that different band members have brought over the years. This is particularly true of the keyboard player position, of course, but also Trevor Rabin's attitude to the guitar differs wildly from that of Steve Howe, which has led to some interesting live interpretations on occasion. Yet a huge proportion of the live recordings are based around the 'classic' lineup of Anderson, Squire, Howe and White plus a keyboard player – most often Rick Wakeman.

This means that live recordings are long on versions of 'And You and I' and 'Roundabout' and somewhat lacking (for instance) 'To Be Over', which is frustrating for many fans like me that revere the latter track as much as its better-known cousins. That's band politics for you.

One final note: in the 1970s, there was a clear division between an official release and a bootleg. In the modern era, the lines are somewhat blurred. The DVD *The Revealing Science of God*, for instance, was recorded for TV in Hungary in 1998 and appeared to buy via official channels like Amazon in 2012. One suspects that the band will not see a penny from this release – yet here it is, available to buy legally and most likely unchallenged.

Many periods of the band's history remain underrepresented as a result. Interestingly, thisdoesn't apply to the Bank's / Kaye era, where the band played a large number of sessions for the BBC. However, the Moraz and *Drama* eras are very lacking in material outside bootlegs, as are the 1988 and 1994 tours with the *90125* lineup, neither of which made it to Europe. As we shall see, if you want footage of the *Union* tour, you're in clover.

Official Recordings – 1973-2001
Beyond and Before (US title) / Something's Coming (UK title) – the BBC Recordings 1969-1970 (CD) 1997

Although not all technically 'live' tracks – BBC sessions often allowed overdubs – these interesting recordings were culled (mainly) from BBC sessions during 1969 and 1970 – around the time of the first two albums. Peter Banks curated this double CD set and wrote the liner notes in 1997. Like Banks' entertaining memoir, also called *Beyond And Before*, his writing is a slightly uncomfortable mix of celebration and bitterness. However, the songs themselves are of varying interest and even more variable sound quality. The usual suspects – in terms of tracks – are there and the variations in arrangements are interesting rather than essential. There are a few gems, though. The trio of 'Looking Around' (recorded in August 1969), 'Sweet Dreams' and 'Then' (both recorded for The Dave Lee Travis Show in January 1970) are terrific, all played lightning-fast without too many embellishments. The arrangement of 'Sweet Dreams' in particular, more than hints at the Beatles at their hardest-rocking, with Anderson pulling out all the stops to sound like Paul McCartney. The live set on CD2 (introduced by John Peel) is classy and features 'For Everyone', discussed earlier with *Time And A Word*.

Yessongs (LP triple album, CD double album) 1973, (Movie/DVD) 1975
As a live act, Yes were probably at their height during the *Close to the Edge* era. Whether Bruford or White were playing drums, the band 'cooked'. They played fast, they were tight and they took chances onstage. Some of Steve Howe's playing, in particular, teeters on the edge of failure, so bold is it. The sheer power that the players generated was frightening. This comes across beautifully in this classic triple album recorded in 1972 and 1973.

The album does have a fabulous 'live' feel and is structured like a long live gig, although Bill Bruford is featured on a few tracks, and the album does include Wakeman, Howe and Squire's live solo pieces. Also, some of the tropes that would become part of Yes live performance for many years to come – Wakeman's stunning Moog solo during 'Wurm' for instance, and Howe's extended guitar improv during 'Yours Is No Disgrace' and here presented for the first time.

Sonically, it is not the best, however, with a raw, back-row-of-the-circle feel to it. How much you enjoy these recordings depends on what you want to take from them, but the performances are jaw-dropping. The triple album format gave Roger Dean the opportunity to let rip with some of his boldest paintings, too.

A 72-minute movie was hastily recorded at the Rainbow in London at roughly the same time as the album and finally released in 1975. The haste shows – it sounds fine but is visually very dark. It is currently available on DVD with a pretty Roger Dean cover. Again, the performances are excellent, Wakeman's cape sparkles attractively, and the visuals also show that not everyone at a Yes show is always played live. Back in those primitive days, Eddie Offord was still able to drop in pre-recorded instruments and sound effects. In 'Close to the Edge', for instance, the church organ is clearly being patched in, allowing Wakeman to play the Moog part.

Yesshows (LP & CD double album) 1979
This was a somewhat more controversial release, made of recordings from various sources between 1976 and 1978 with both Moraz and Wakeman. There was some injudicious editing to make the album flow better and had 'Ritual' uncomfortably covering most of two sides of vinyl. Mixed by Squire, not all of the band liked the mixes at a time when the 'classic' lineup was on its last legs anyway. It's actually pretty good, though, and most notable for a searing version of 'Gates of Delirium'. I have always liked the Roger Dean cover – less busy than many, with a single bird flying over mountain tops through a wispy blue sky.There are some clunky moments – the false segue from 'Time and a Word' going into 'Going For The One' being the obvious one. The recordings were taken for different tours, not just different shows. Additionally, with the album representing a concerted effort not to reuse material from *Yessongs,* it feels a lot less like a live gig and a lot more like a bunch of tracks stuck together for convenience.

9012Live (VHS, DVD, CD & LP) 1985
Recorded in 1984 on the 90125 tour, this is glossy, professional, effects-laden stuff, although later DVD versions of the recording offer a video mix without the rather kitsch visual effects. It's all dated terribly. The performances – showcasing Rabin's guitar and the somewhat hideous 1980s stage outfits – are excellent, however. It's worth finding if you can. The live mini-album – *9012Live The Solos* – is far less interesting. It features some 'you really had to be there' solo moments from all five band members and good live versions of 'Hold on' and 'Changes'. CD versions are rare but available for completists. I am happy with my vinyl copy, thanks.

The Keys to Ascension (VHS, DVD, 4 CDs) 1996
Now it gets complicated! Recorded in San Luis Obispo, California (Anderson's charming home town), in 1996, following the return of Howe and Wakeman, the concerts were released on VHS but quickly withdrawn due to quality issues. A DVD was issued in 2005. Although the setlist itself is not without

interest – there are live versions of 'The Revealing Science of God', 'Turn of the Century' and 'Onward', for instance – the music is decent rather than essential. Steve Howe has discussed working hard on the tapes himself to make them acceptable. The visual effects, however, are ill-judged and distracting. The live music appeared across the two *Keys to Ascension* double albums that also included the new material already discussed. Overall, a confusing and rather unsatisfactory package. The live versions are unlikely to be played much, even by diehard fans.

Live from the House of Blues (DVD and double CD as House of Yes) 2001

The band's first purpose-shot DVD – with Billy Sherwood alongside Howe on guitar and vocals and Igor Khoroshev on keyboards – this recording marks the end (in my opinion) of the band as an active recording/touring outfit. Showcasing *The Ladder* album and without any extended solo sequences, this is actually rather good, with Khoroshev's virtuosity allowing the band to play Wakeman material with conviction. 'Awaken' is particularly impressive. Hereafter, the band have concentrated largely on older material even when promoting new albums.

The New Millennium

As already mentioned, *Live From the House of Blues* marks the transition from Yes as a recording/touring unit to Yes, effectively, as a heritage band. Although there were three new studio albums in this period – at time of writing – the amount of live product put out by the band in this time was phenomenal.

There is very little here – except perhaps some of the bootleg quality releases that do not have band approval – that is poor in quality, yet also very little that is essential. While it's pleasant to see the band in its dotage run through those great pieces from the 1970s, there are few performances here that you need to see or hear above versions that are already available. Indeed, since the early 2000s, many fans have been complaining of slowing tempos – as the older material becomes harder to play with ageing fingers and limbs.

Initially, the increase in sales of DVDs (later the better-quality Blurays) saw this as the main medium for releasing live material. However, online streaming led to a massive drop in DVD sales, so most of the releases chronicled here were bolstered by later CD releases. Indeed, since around 2010, the fashion has been for joint releases, typically a double CD set and a 'bonus' DVD with the same show presented without bells and whistles. The fashion to focus live shows around whole album performances has also facilitated this. In no particular order, then:

The Word is Live (triple CD) 2005

This beautifully-curated boxed set of CDs for fans, fills in many of the gaps in live performance, particularly the early Peter Banks years, and the Patrick

Moraz era – there is a searing version of 'Sound Chaser'. The *Drama* period is also covered, as is the *Big Generator* Tour. The rarer tracks are discussed as they come up earlier in this book. Be warned that many of the pieces on this set are little better than good bootleg standard of interest to fans for their historical aspects rather than for their pristine, hifi qualities.

The Lost Broadcasts (DVD) 2009
Released in various versions over the years, these TV broadcasts (from German and Belgian TV) from 1969 to 1971 feature both Banks and Howe and are fascinating viewing for fans of the early band, particularly those that are particularly interested – as I am – in the early contribution of Tony Kaye to the band's sound.

Symphonic Live (double DVD, double CD) 2002
An excellent package presenting the 2001 *Symphonic* Tour with full orchestra and the excellent Tom Brislin on keyboards. This was a very special, joyous tour, and given the excellent use of a full orchestra, it's an opportunity to hear and see very different versions of some Yes epics. If you are short on cash and looking for one DVD to buy, this might just be the right one.

Union Live (double DVD, double CD) 2011
Another great package compiled by Voiceprint, chronicling the 1991 *Union* tour from various sources – in varying quality.

Yes – Live 1975 at QPR (Laserdisc)
This must be the most frustrating Yes release in history. Available in many formats over the years, but never officially, this superb – nearly three hour – concert, shot at Loftus Road (home of London soccer club QPR) in 1975, was filmed by the BBC for the *Old Grey Whistle Test*. The visuals – and performance – are great, but only the portion broadcast has been mixed properly, which means that the audio is terrible for a lot of the concert. Nonetheless, as a historical document of the Moraz era, it's worth finding if you can.

Anderson, Bruford, Wakeman, Howe – An Evening of Yes Music Plus (DVD and double CD) 1993 and 2006
This is not a Yes recording per se, but it is interesting for the high quality of the Yes tracks the band played on the tour, particularly a superb 'Close to the Edge'. Bruford's electronic percussion also adds an interesting, if dated, texture.

Yesspeak (double DVD) 2003
Narrated by Roger Daltrey and recorded 20 years ago, this double DVD set mixes lengthy interviews with the five members of the then-band – Anderson, Squire, Howe, White, Wakeman – with live footage, mainly from a show in

Birmingham on the 2003 tour, attended by the author. Interesting though the interviews are, they have been rendered obsolete over time, and fans complained that there wasn't enough live footage, which led to ...

The New Directors Cut (double DVD) 2008
This excised most of the interviews and instead features the entire Birmingham concert – which is excellent – with rather less inspiring footage of the band at the Glastonbury Festival, UK, in July 2003.

Live at Montreux (DVD, CD) 2003
Another – albeit shortened – version of the 2003 set. It has decent enough visuals and sound and is particularly good for lovers of close-ups.

Acoustic – Guaranteed No Hiss (DVD) 2004
A short, entertaining acoustic set, broadcast live in cinemas across the USA in January 2004. The band enjoyed this performance, and it became the basis for the acoustic set on the 2004 world tour. Again, it's worth picking up for some of the interesting – if hardly essential – live versions played on acoustic instruments. Wakeman looks the most comfortable, given his skill on the piano.

Songs from Tsongas (double DVD & double CD) 2004
After the hugely successful reunion tour in 2003, the band stepped it up in 2004, playing bigger venues and a longer set, including a mid-concert acoustic performance. This gig from the USA is a decent chronicle of a good performance at the end of the US leg of the tour.

In the Present – Live from Lyon (double CD) 2009
An interesting document of the Benoît David / Oliver Wakeman period of the band, and nicely performed all round. The package was reissued in 2019 as part of the *From A Page* box set with one extra track, part of Howe's acoustic set.

Like it is – at Bristol Hippodrome (double CD, DVD, Blu-ray) 2014
Like it is – at the Mesa Arts Centre (double CD, DVD, Blu-ray) 2015
These companion sets feature the four albums that the band were playing in their entirety around this time – *The Yes Album, Fragile, Close to the Edge* and *Going for the One*. Although the band – including Jon Davidson and Geoff Downes – do a decent job, these albums really are non-essential, even if the Mesa Arts Centre gig does, sadly, feature Chris Squire's last recorded work.

Progeny – Seven Shows from 1972 (14 CDs) 2015
Progeny – Highlights from 1972 (double CD) 2016
This remarkable, lovingly compiled package features seven shows from autumn 1972 – with identical sets – on the US leg of the *Close to the Edge*

tour. Offering better sound quality than *Yessongs*, it's an invaluable addition to the catalogue, recorded at a time when the band were probably at their best as a live unit, with Howe really taking chances in his playing. I have the highlights version, and that's enough for me, but die-hard fans may want to revel in the subtle differences between each of the seven shows.

The Revealing Science of God (DVD) 2010
A poor-quality recording of a Hungarian TV broadcast from 1998. Of historical rather than aesthetic interest, it does include live versions of 'The Revealing Science Of God' and 'America'.

Live in Philadelphia 1979 (DVD) 1996
Poor-quality visuals typify this brief – 51 minute – snippet of a show from 1979. It does, however, give a good perspective on the innovative 'in the round' stage from the 1978-79 world tour.

Topographic Drama (double CD) 2017
These live recordings – featuring *Drama* and parts of *Tales from Topographic Oceans* were the first to be made following the death of Chris Squire and the illness of Alan White, so the drum stool is taken by Jay Schellen for the majority of the album, White only appearing for the end of 'Ritual' and the encores.

Billy Sherwood does an excellent job with Squire's bass parts, although his voice is a little less distinctive as a harmony vocalist. Watching him play *Drama* (and *Fragile*) in the UK, it became clear how difficult – and physical – Squire's bass parts were, and how easy Chris made it look, even in his mid-60s. Again, however, these are non-essential live recordings, although Jon Davison, as ever, makes both a fine Jon Anderson and Trevor Horn.

Yes Featuring Jon Anderson, Trevor Rabin and Rick Wakeman – Live at the Apollo (double CD, Blu-ray, DVD) 2018
All of a sudden, in 2017, there were two Yes's. With the Howe / White / Squire version of the band working pretty much constantly throughout the 2010s, it took over five years for Anderson to fully recover his strength after his near-death experience in 2008. A tour with Rick Wakeman in 2011 showed him looking frail and singing well enough without having the power to pull off full band shows. However, announcements that he was planning to record and tour with Wakeman and Trevor Rabin caused some excitement. With small arena / large theatre dates finally booked for late 2016 and early 2017- around the same time that Yes were playing theatres. The battle – albeit a polite one – was on. Initially billing themselves by their names only, the Yes moniker with name qualifiers was adopted in early 2017. The band had no rights to use the Roger Dean logo.

This audio and video package – available in most formats, as is the fashion these days – was exciting for featuring Anderson in exceptionally good voice at a then 73 and for the rarity of hearing Wakeman's florid keyboard style on Rabin era songs, although classic Yes was also well represented. With Lee Pomeroy (a long-time Wakeman cohort) on bass and Louis Molino III on drums (brought in by Rabin), the band even dared to slightly rearrange pieces like 'Awaken'. Of all the late 2010-era Yes live offerings, this is probably the most interesting, but beware of the distracting dubbed-on crowd noise.

Live At Glastonbury Festival 2003 (Double CD) 2020

The set already seen on video as the New Directors Cut was finally released on licence on a double CD in early 2020. It's not bad, but the lack of preparation and soundcheck time at the event comes across in the stand-alone audio. The CDs also feature four tracks that appeared on a different DVD, Yes Acoustic.

Yes 50 Live (2019) (Double CD, Triple album)

To celebrate the 50th-anniversary world tour which took place in 2018, the band released another live package. In the main, this was well-received, and it did allow them to feature a few rare pieces such as 'Madrigal', 'Nine Voices' and 'We Can Fly From Here Part One'. The album also featured appearances from Tony Kaye and Patrick Moraz. As usual, one does wonder how many live versions of 'Close To The Edge' and 'Roundabout' we really need. But it's a decent package with great artwork from Roger Dean.

The Royal Affair Tour – Live From Las Vegas (CD, Double Vinyl album) 2020

In October 2020, yet another live album appeared, this time from the 'Royal Affair' North American tour in 2019. As usual, the recording quality was excellent, even if the track selection itself was less than inspiring. With 'Gates Of Delirium', held back for a live album from the planned *Relayer* tour in 2021 (which never took place), the only crumbs of comfort were a live version of the rarely-performed 'No Opportunity Necessary, No Experience Needed' and a saccharine cover of John Lennon's 'Imagine', which was also released as a stand-alone digital single.

Yes Union 30 Live (26 CDs, 4 DVDs) 2021

This sumptuous and very expensive boxed set presented a new mix of the *Union* Shoreline Amphiteater show. It then pads out a huge, celebratory set with former bootleg material of very variable quality. Many fans cried 'foul' and refused to pay the massive price for what was deemed substandard. Your correspondent was one that didn't bite, so I can't comment on the content myself, but it's clearly non-essential.

Bibliography

The following books are either essential or useful reading about Yes:

Banks, P., James B., *Beyond And Before – The Formative Years Of Yes* (Golden Treasures Publishing, 2001)

Martin, B., *Music Of Yes – Structure And Vision In Progressive Rock* (Open Court, 1996)

Welch, C., *Close To The Edge – The Story Of Yes* (Omnibus Press, 1998)

Popoff, M., *Time and a Word – The Yes Story* (Soundcheck Books, 2016)

Watkinson, D., *Yes – Perpetual Change* (Plexus, 2001)

Bruford, W., *The Autobiography* (Jawbone, 2009)

Romano, W., *Close To The Edge* (Backbeat, 2017)

O'Reilly, S., *Yes And Philosophy* (Self Published, 2012)

Morse, T., *Yes Stories – Yes In Their Own Words* (St. Martin's Griffin, 1996)

Chambers, S., Yes – An Endless Dream Of '70s, '80s And '90s Rock Music (General Store, 2002)

Farley, A., *The Extraordinary World Of Yes* (iUniverse Inc, 2004)

Kirkman, J., *Time And A Word* – The Yes Interviews (Easy On The Eye Books, 2018)

Wakeman, R., *Say Yes* (Hodder And Stoughton, 1995)

Lambe, S with Watkinson, D., *Yes in the 1980s* (Sonicbond Publishing, 2021)

Mulryne, K., *Yes. The Tormato Story* (Self Published, 2023)

The following more general books on Progressive Rock also give some insight into Yes:

Macan, E., *Rocking The Classics* (OUP, 1997)

Romano, W., *Mountains Come Out Of The Sky* (Backbeat, 2010)

Snider, C., *The Strawberry Bricks Guide To Progressive Rock* (Lulu, 2008)

Stump, P., *The Music's All That Matters* (Quartet, 1997)

Lambe,S., *Citizens Of Hope And Glory – The Story Of Progressive Rock* (Amberley, 2011)

Ewing, J., *Wonderous Stories – A Journey Through The Landscape Of Progressive Rock* (Flood Gallery, 2018)

Online resources

yesworld.com – the official Yes website

yesfeaturingarw.com – official website of the Anderson, Rabin, Wakeman version of the band

yesfans.com – long running fan site and forum

yesmusicpodcast.com – excellent weekly podcast about the band

bondegezou.co.uk – website of long-term Yes chronicler Henry Potts

forgotten-yesterdays.com – invaluable online resource

Facebook has many Yes related groups. Join them at your leisure (or indeed peril).

Also available from Sonicbond

On Track series

Allman Brothers Band – Andrew Wild
978-1-78952-252-5
Tori Amos – Lisa Torem 978-1-78952-142-9
Aphex Twin – Beau Waddell 978-1-78952-267-9
Asia – Peter Braidis 978-1-78952-099-6
Badfinger – Robert Day-Webb 978-1-878952-176-4
Barclay James Harvest – Keith and Monica Domone
978-1-78952-067-5
Beck – Arthur Lizie 978-1-78952-258-7
The Beatles – Andrew Wild 978-1-78952-009-5
The Beatles Solo 1969-1980 – Andrew Wild
978-1-78952-030-9
Blue Oyster Cult – Jacob Holm-Lupo
978-1-78952-007-1
Blur – Matt Bishop 978-178952-164-1
Marc Bolan and T.Rex – Peter Gallagher
978-1-78952-124-5
Kate Bush – Bill Thomas 978-1-78952-097-2
Camel – Hamish Kuzminski 978-1-78952-040-8
Captain Beefheart – Opher Goodwin
978-1-78952-235-8
Caravan – Andy Boot 978-1-78952-127-6
Cardiacs – Eric Benac 978-1-78952-131-3
Nick Cave and The Bad Seeds – Dominic Sanderson
978-1-78952-240-2
Eric Clapton Solo – Andrew Wild 978-1-78952-141-2
The Clash – Nick Assirati 978-1-78952-077-4
Elvis Costello and The Attractions – Georg Purvis
978-1-78952-129-0
Crosby, Stills and Nash – Andrew Wild
978-1-78952-039-2
Creedence Clearwater Revival – Tony Thompson
978-178952-237-2
The Damned – Morgan Brown 978-1-78952-136-8
Deep Purple and Rainbow 1968-79 – Steve Pilkington
978-1-78952-002-6
Dire Straits – Andrew Wild 978-1-78952-044-6
The Doors – Tony Thompson 978-1-78952-137-5
Dream Theater – Jordan Blum 978-1-78952-050-7
Eagles – John Van der Kiste 978-1-78952-260-0
Earth, Wind and Fire – Bud Wilkins
978-1-78952-272-3
Electric Light Orchestra – Barry Delve
978-1-78952-152-8
Emerson Lake and Palmer – Mike Goode
978-1-78952-000-2
Fairport Convention – Kevan Furbank
978-1-78952-051-4
Peter Gabriel – Graeme Scarfe 978-1-78952-138-2
Genesis – Stuart MacFarlane 978-1-78952-005-7
Gentle Giant – Gary Steel 978-1-78952-058-3
Gong – Kevan Furbank 978-1-78952-082-8
Green Day – William E. Spevack 978-1-78952-261-7
Hall and Oates – Ian Abrahams 978-1-78952-167-2
Hawkwind – Duncan Harris 978-1-78952-052-1
Peter Hammill – Richard Rees Jones
978-1-78952-163-4
Roy Harper – Opher Goodwin 978-1-78952-130-6
Jimi Hendrix – Emma Stott 978-1-78952-175-7
The Hollies – Andrew Darlington 978-1-78952-159-7
Horslips – Richard James 978-1-78952-263-1
The Human League and The Sheffield Scene –

Andrew Darlington 978-1-78952-186-3
The Incredible String Band – Tim Moon
978-1-78952-107-8
Iron Maiden – Steve Pilkington 978-1-78952-061-3
Joe Jackson – Richard James 978-1-78952-189-4
Jefferson Airplane – Richard Butterworth
978-1-78952-143-6
Jethro Tull – Jordan Blum 978-1-78952-016-3
Elton John in the 1970s – Peter Kearns
978-1-78952-034-7
Billy Joel – Lisa Torem 978-1-78952-183-2
Judas Priest – John Tucker 978-1-78952-018-7
Kansas – Kevin Cummings 978-1-78952-057-6
The Kinks – Martin Hutchinson 978-1-78952-172-6
Korn – Matt Karpe 978-1-78952-153-5
Led Zeppelin – Steve Pilkington 978-1-78952-151-1
Level 42 – Matt Philips 978-1-78952-102-3
Little Feat – Georg Purvis - 978-1-78952-168-9
Aimee Mann – Jez Rowden 978-1-78952-036-1
Joni Mitchell – Peter Kearns 978-1-78952-081-1
The Moody Blues – Geoffrey Feakes
978-1-78952-042-2
Motorhead – Duncan Harris 978-1-78952-173-3
Nektar – Scott Meze – 978-1-78952-257-0
New Order – Dennis Remmer – 978-1-78952-249-5
Nightwish – Simon McMurdo – 978-1-78952-270-9
Laura Nyro – Philip Ward 978-1-78952-182-5
Mike Oldfield – Ryan Yard 978-1-78952-060-6
Opeth – Jordan Blum 978-1-78-952-166-5
Pearl Jam – Ben L. Connor 978-1-78952-188-7
Tom Petty – Richard James 978-1-78952-128-3
Pink Floyd – Richard Butterworth 978-1-78952-242-6
The Police – Pete Braidis 978-1-78952-158-0
Porcupine Tree – Nick Holmes 978-1-78952-144-3
Queen – Andrew Wild 978-1-78952-003-3
Radiohead – William Allen 978-1-78952-149-8
Rancid – Paul Matts 989-1-78952-187-0
Renaissance – David Detmer 978-1-78952-062-0
REO Speedwagon – Jim Romag 978-1-78952-262-4
The Rolling Stones 1963-80 – Steve Pilkington
978-1-78952-017-0
The Smiths and Morrissey – Tommy Gunnarsson
978-1-78952-140-5
Spirit – Rev. Keith A. Gordon – 978-1-78952- 248-8
Stackridge – Alan Draper 978-1-78952-232-7
Status Quo the Frantic Four Years – Richard James
978-1-78952-160-3
Steely Dan – Jez Rowden 978-1-78952-043-9
Steve Hackett – Geoffrey Feakes 978-1-78952-098-9
Tears For Fears – Paul Clark - 978-178952-238-9
Thin Lizzy – Graeme Stroud 978-1-78952-064-4
Tool – Matt Karpe 978-1-78952-234-1
Toto – Jacob Holm-Lupo 978-1-78952-019-4
U2 – Eoghan Lyng 978-1-78952-078-1
UFO – Richard James 978-1-78952-073-6
Van Der Graaf Generator – Dan Coffey
978-1-78952-031-6
Van Halen – Morgan Brown – 9781-78952-256-3
The Who – Geoffrey Feakes 978-1-78952-076-7
Roy Wood and the Move – James R Turner
978-1-78952-008-8
Yes – Stephen Lambe 978-1-78952-001-9
Frank Zappa 1966 to 1979 – Eric Benac

978-1-78952-033-0
Warren Zevon – Peter Gallagher 978-1-78952-170-2
10CC – Peter Kearns 978-1-78952-054-5

Decades Series
The Bee Gees in the 1960s – Andrew Mon Hughes et al
978-1-78952-148-1
The Bee Gees in the 1970s – Andrew Mon Hughes et al
978-1-78952-179-5
Black Sabbath in the 1970s – Chris Sutton
978-1-78952-171-9
Britpop – Peter Richard Adams and Matt Pooler
978-1-78952-169-6
Phil Collins in the 1980s – Andrew Wild
978-1-78952-185-6
Alice Cooper in the 1970s – Chris Sutton
978-1-78952-104-7
Alice Cooper in the 1980s – Chris Sutton
978-1-78952-259-4
Curved Air in the 1970s – Laura Shenton
978-1-78952-069-9
Donovan in the 1960s – Jeff Fitzgerald
978-1-78952-233-4
Bob Dylan in the 1980s – Don Klees
978-1-78952-157-3
Brian Eno in the 1970s – Gary Parsons
978-1-78952-239-6
Faith No More in the 1990s – Matt Karpe
978-1-78952-250-1
Fleetwood Mac in the 1970s – Andrew Wild
978-1-78952-105-4
Fleetwood Mac in the 1980s – Don Klees
978-178952-254-9
Focus in the 1970s – Stephen Lambe
978-1-78952-079-8
Free and Bad Company in the 1970s – John Van der
Kiste 978-1-78952-178-8
Genesis in the 1970s – Bill Thomas 978178952-146-7
George Harrison in the 1970s – Eoghan Lyng
978-1-78952-174-0
Kiss in the 1970s – Peter Gallagher 978-1-78952-246-4
Manfred Mann's Earth Band in the 1970s – John Van
der Kiste 978178952-243-3
Marillion in the 1980s – Nathaniel Webb
978-1-78952-065-1
Van Morrison in the 1970s – Peter Childs -
978-1-78952-241-9
Mott the Hoople and Ian Hunter in the 1970s –
John Van der Kiste 978-1-78-952-162-7
Pink Floyd In The 1970s – Georg Purvis
978-1-78952-072-9
Suzi Quatro in the 1970s – Darren Johnson
978-1-78952-236-5
Queen in the 1970s – James Griffiths
978-1-78952-265-5
Roxy Music in the 1970s – Dave Thompson
978-1-78952-180-1
Slade in the 1970s – Darren Johnson
978-1-78952-268-6

Status Quo in the 1980s – Greg Harper
978-1-78952-244-0
Tangerine Dream in the 1970s – Stephen Palmer
978-1-78952-161-0
The Sweet in the 1970s – Darren Johnson
978-1-78952-139-9
Uriah Heep in the 1970s – Steve Pilkington
978-1-78952-103-0
Van der Graaf Generator in the 1970s –
Steve Pilkington 978-1-78952-245-7
Rick Wakeman in the 1970s – Geoffrey Feakes
978-1-78952-264-8
Yes in the 1980s – Stephen Lambe with
David Watkinson 978-1-78952-125-2

On Screen series
Carry On… – Stephen Lambe 978-1-78952-004-0
David Cronenberg – Patrick Chapman
978-1-78952-071-2
Doctor Who: The David Tennant Years – Jamie
Hailstone 978-1-78952-066-8
James Bond – Andrew Wild 978-1-78952-010-1
Monty Python – Steve Pilkington 978-1-78952-047-7
Seinfeld Seasons 1 to 5 – Stephen Lambe
978-1-78952-012-5

Other Books
1967: A Year In Psychedelic Rock 978-1-78952-155-9
1970: A Year In Rock – John Van der Kiste
978-1-78952-147-4
1973: The Golden Year of Progressive Rock
978-1-78952-165-8
Babysitting A Band On The Rocks – G.D. Praetorius
978-1-78952-106-1
Eric Clapton Sessions – Andrew Wild
978-1-78952-177-1
Derek Taylor: For Your Radioactive Children –
Andrew Darlington 978-1-78952-038-5
The Golden Road: The Recording History of The
Grateful Dead – John Kilbride 978-1-78952-156-6
Iggy and The Stooges On Stage 1967-1974 –
Per Nilsen 978-1-78952-101-6
Jon Anderson and the Warriors – the road to Yes –
David Watkinson 978-1-78952-059-0
Magic: The David Paton Story – David Paton
978-1-78952-266-2
Misty: The Music of Johnny Mathis – Jakob Baekgaard
978-1-78952-247-1
Nu Metal: A Definitive Guide – Matt Karpe
978-1-78952-063-7
Tommy Bolin: In and Out of Deep Purple – Laura
Shenton 978-1-78952-070-5
Maximum Darkness – Deke Leonard
978-1-78952-048-4
The Twang Dynasty – Deke Leonard
978-1-78952-049-1

and many more to come!

Would you like to write for Sonicbond Publishing?

At Sonicbond Publishing we are always on the look-out for authors, particularly for our two main series:

On Track. Mixing fact with in depth analysis, the On Track series examines the work of a particular musical artist or group. All genres are considered from easy listening and jazz to 60s soul to 90s pop, via rock and metal.

On Screen. This series looks at the world of film and television. Subjects considered include directors, actors and writers, as well as entire television and film series. As with the On Track series, we balance fact with analysis.

While professional writing experience would, of course, be an advantage the most important qualification is to have real enthusiasm and knowledge of your subject. First-time authors are welcomed, but the ability to write well in English is essential.

Sonicbond Publishing has distribution throughout Europe and North America, and all books are also published in E-book form. Authors will be paid a royalty based on sales of their book.

Further details are available from www.sonicbondpublishing.co.uk. To contact us, complete the contact form there or
email info@sonicbondpublishing.co.uk